W9-AMP-574

WINDOWS ON THE WORKPLACE

WINDOWS ON THE WORKPLACE

Computers, Jobs, and the Organization of Office Work in the Late Twentieth Century

JOAN GREENBAUM

**MONTHLY REVIEW PRESS
NEW YORK**

**To Harriet Held Greenbaum and Nathan Greenbaum
who taught me to read between the lines**

Copyright © 1995 by Joan Greenbaum
All rights reserved

Library of Congress Cataloging-in-Publication Data

   Windows on the workplace : computers, jobs, and the organization of office work
in the late twentieth century / by Joan Greenbaum.
       p.   cm.
   Incudes bibliographical references and index.
   ISBN 0-85345-900-2 : $22.00. — ISBN 0-85345-901-0 (pbk.) : $10.00
   1. Office practice—Automation. 2. Employees—Effect of automation on. 3.
Labor supply—Effect of automation on.
I. Title.
HF5548.G717   1995
651.8—dc20   94-31725
                                                                     CIP

Monthly Review Press
122 West 27th Street
New York, NY 10001

Manufactured in the United States of America
10 9 8 7 6 5 4 3 2 1

CONTENTS

PREFACE

In 1966 I moved to New York and landed a job as a programmer at IBM. Getting a job as a programmer at that time generally required some college (I had a bachelor's degree in economics), some luck with a thing called the Programmer Aptitude Test (I worked with a placement agency that taught me how to take the test), and what someone called "passing the mirror test" (if they held a mirror to your nose and it fogged up, you were hired). This situation was quite different from today, when thousands of applicants with graduate degrees in computer science are competing for a limited number of good jobs.

I worked as a programmer, analyst, project manager, and consultant up through the early 1970s, when in an attempt to figure out how computers were being used to affect jobs, I went into academia to study political economy. There were two adages of the day that still stick in my mind and that are repeated like mantras by talk-show hosts and as leads in newspaper columns.

The first argues that technology makes workers more productive, while the second optimistically tells us that technology creates more jobs than it replaces.

But to me commonsense dictated that if workers are made more productive by technology, fewer of them will be needed. And if fewer workers are needed, how can more jobs be created? I itched to use my knowledge about how computer systems were designed to peel away the high-tech glitter surrounding such critical issues.

These issues are usually circumvented by arguments that ask us to take a long historical view. Journalists and researchers alike refer us back to the early automobile era and point out that even though blacksmiths were replaced, there have been more jobs in auto production, repair, and highway construction. Such arguments are comforting, but they sidestep the more complex issues, covering them over with the language of job "displacement," which makes it seem that while some jobs will be displaced, new ones will always be created. To be sure, the example of black-smiths and auto production illustrates job displacement, and replacement, at the turn of the last century. But as we enter the next century, it is clear that there aren't all that many places where displaced auto assembly-line workers can go when auto production is sped up by robotics and new forms of work organization. Nor are there jobs for former gas station attendants and mechanics, who are not needed as customers are expected to pump their own gas, or as electronic parts are designed to be thrown away and replaced by new ones rather than fiddled with by mechanics. Some tell us that this is not a problem since the new "information superhighway" will generate new jobs by creating new services. But as the stories, examples, and data in this book will show, white-collar jobs—the backbone of the so-called information society and a key pillar of the information highway—are not showing any strong growth trends, certainly not enough to absorb those workers "displaced" out of other jobs.

As we stand at the turn of the twenty-first century being

bombarded with statements like, "Led by innovations in technology ..." or "Progress and technology are what has kept America great," it is almost as if we are expected to believe that a constant repetition of these slogans makes them true—a sort of technological leap of faith. Instead, we need to reshape the debate in order to have a clear picture of what we can do.

In 1993, *Business Week*, among other magazines, announced that computer technology was finally making workers more productive, but that it wasn't just the technology that had made this happen, it was also the way business managers were choosing to restructure work, using technology to do so. The business press, having heralded the coming of productivity, now announced its arrival. But while technology may indeed be used to make workers more productive, the assertion that technology creates jobs remains more elusive. There is no way to prove or disprove that technology creates more jobs than it replaces, and this book will not attempt to do so. Indeed, a central premise here is that technology is designed to blend in with and support top management's objectives, including work organization and business restructuring, thus making no clear dividing line between a "technical" change and an organizational one.

From this perspective, it is not technology that stands at the center of change. But to debunk the myth of technology we need to look more closely at work and the meaning of work and jobs.

For many people, work and the workplace carry meanings beyond the obvious need for financial security. Particularly in America, the work ethic drives the culture so completely that "What do you do?" is a form of social greeting. Work means a place to go. It also means a social group, a clique of friends or colleagues to talk to. Many people identify to some degree with their work; they want to do a good job and feel good about it. By taking pride in work, they come away with a sense of self-respect. And many people, in trying to work to their potential, have invested something of themselves in education, training, and on-the-job experience.

Yet jobs are changing. There is less security in having a job now than there was a decade ago. More and more jobs are temporary or contracted out for short periods of time. Competition for jobs increases as more and more people complete more years of schooling and the number of full-time jobs matching their specific qualifications decreases. Many people think it is only happening to them. At kitchen tables, in living rooms, or out at social gatherings, they talk tentatively about how they seem to be having trouble finding a good job—one like the job they used to have or want to get. There is much talk about how their company may have "downsized" them, or how a particular manager was too stupid to stop the moves that the company was making, or how their company unfortunately got stuck in a bad market or bad merger. Recent high school and college graduates wonder if they had studied something different or perhaps lived in a different place, there would be more opportunities.

These people are not alone. The changes being made to jobs are affecting a wide range of workers, from recent graduates to those being pushed toward early retirement. During the feminist movement of the 1960s and 1970s, we used to say that the "personal is political." This expression clearly applies to the workforce: what people are experiencing as a personal problem is a deeply rooted and broad-ranging political one. There is a whole lot of victim-blaming going on, and this effectively isolates people rather than allowing them to come forward and find out what they can do together. Even the creation of terms like "computer illiterate" makes people believe that it is somehow their fault that they have been left out of the televised version of a high-tech society. Yet it is no more possible to be computer illiterate than it is to be telephone illiterate, for using computer applications, like using telephones, depends mainly on knowing the task that you are doing. Pushing the right buttons follows.

This book is written as a small road away from high-tech glitter and toward a place where we can find ways to make better choices. You won't find an on ramp to the information superhighway here, although you will find an analysis of how computer systems are being designed to change the way we work. And you will find research, stories, examples, and historical analysis that will hopefully help us look more clearly out of windows that are not clouded by overly optimistic and misleading visions.

The software program called Windows, in widespread use, has in some ways become a metaphor for the 1990s. I too have chosen the "windows" metaphor for the title of this book. Windows can both open and close; they can let in light or have curtains drawn across them; they can open to a view or look out on blank walls. A window, in and of itself, does not say anything about what is beyond it, but it offers possibilities.

This book is also about analysis and action. If we use analytical tools to dig more deeply into issues, we will be able to choose alternative courses of action. Looking optimistically toward the future doesn't help us learn from the past. Nor does it help us find the road that we want to be on in the present. If we are going to create paths to alternative futures and shape realistic social choices, we need to move beyond the "talk-show version" of contemporary life. Social choice, including technological choice, can take many forms. It can come in the shape of community group programs, workplace associations, professional groups, unions, and governmental legislation. Whatever we choose requires more than a technological leap of faith.

There were many people who were enormously helpful in making this book come together. Bill Tabb, with insight and clear criticism, was a positive force in getting me started and telling me how to stop. Sharon Szymanski helped me talk my way through logical inconsistencies and Cydney Pullman reminded me how to keep on track. And in her usual supportive and inspirational role, Sandy Watson urged me on and said that it was important. Danny Lynch, whose poem appears as an epilogue, asked critical questions and made helpful suggestions. Susan Leigh Starr read the manuscript and reminded me about what needed saying while Lucy Suchman reminded me that it needed to be said. In Norway, Tone Bratteteig kept me focused on the central international job issues of the day. And here at home, Sheila Crowell and Ellen Kolba of the Writer's Room at the Montclair Public Schools, offered supportive comments that got me back to the computer keyboard to try to shape the ideas more clearly.

This book was researched and written over a period of two years during which changes in jobs and technology seemed to be coming faster than they had in the past. Susan Lowes, my editor, pushed and pulled me along in the midst of what could have been a researcher's nightmare. In particular she is a genius at asking the kind of questions that one needs to be reminded of. Also at Monthly Review Press, Renee Pendergrass was helpful in her enthusiasm for getting me started and Akiko Ichikawa for her insights in helping me bring the book to a close, as well as in selecting pictures to round out the historical patterns.

Most authors thank one person for efforts above and beyond the call of duty and for me, this person is my son Bart Greenbaum. Not only did he read and reread the manuscript in various (not always very readable) forms, but he commented, argued, and made suggestions from the vantage point of his generation. Although we probably still disagree about what should be done about jobs and technological change, Bart, like his brothers Brian and Jesse, are part of a generation that is deeply affected by these changes and, as a result, will face important decisions.

—Joan Greenbaum
Montclair, New Jersey
May 1995

1

THROUGH THE LOOKING GLASS

"Everyone seems to want everything faxed to them yesterday."
—Office worker, 1995

Office work has changed a great deal over the last thirty years, but the pace of change increased to a gallop in the 1990s. Like the Red Queen in Lewis Carroll's *Through the Looking Glass*, people seem to be running faster and faster to stay in the same place. The media portrays changes in the workplace, particularly in offices, as the progress of high tech, making it seem as if "advances in technology" are inevitably leading to more and better jobs. Yet things are not always what they seem.

Obviously, workers who have had computers and other office technology plunked down on their desks have reason to believe that "advances in technology" have changed their working lives.

But new pieces of office equipment don't simply arrive in peoples' cubicles. What is commonly lumped together as technology—everything from voice mail through software programs to networks—is specifically designed to fit in with management policies to cut labor costs and speed up processing. Managerial objectives, and the technology designed to support them, are propelled along by a number of developments that are frequently clustered around the theme of increased global competition. In the name of meeting the competition and decreasing costs, companies are taking steps to "reengineer" the workplace so that fewer people can do more work for less money.

Reengineered workplaces take many forms. Throughout the book, we will see how developments since the 1950s have led to the workplace of today. In the following example, the large metropolitan newspaper where George works had been bought by a multinational media firm. When he purchased the newspaper, the new owner made it clear not only that he wanted to break the newspaper unions, but that he was intent on standardizing the newspaper process, producing tabloid stories that were of high reader interest but were low on traditional newspaper research techniques.

George is the deputy city editor of the newspaper.[1] The offices are almost soundless. George makes himself walk over and talk to the reporters when he assigns them stories, but this is not what is generally done: most people send each other email messages, while reporters and editors send completed stories from computer to computer.

George has been in the newspaper business for more than twenty years. "I could spend a whole day now without any voice conversation with reporters. I could do my job sitting at home with a modem, fax, and computer. I can't explain what a story needs via email as well as I can in person, but that's the way it's done today." "Story conferences," the meetings where editors and reporters discussed news items and planned how to cover them, have been cut out.

Gone as well is the switchboard, where cub reporters got practice answering phones and passing on important messages. "I hate voice mail," George says, "because you need a human to interpret a message. Like how the hell are you supposed to go after "hot tips" if the caller can only leave a message on your machine?" "Management is thrilled," he adds, "because they can continue to cut staff."

It's particularly irritating to the reporters that the voice-messaging system "automatically" puts incoming calls into voice mail when the reporters are on another call. George explains: "This is a business where you have to have a line open for someone to call you back. But the minute you pick up the phone to make a call, the next call goes into the so-called voice-message place." He compares this voice-mail problem to the "pain of a computer system" that was set up to eliminate typographers and in the process messed up editing by changing the rewriting process. "It's another case of engineering winning out over the editorial process," he says.

Proponents of "high tech" tell us that offices like George's are the wave of the future. The fact that George doesn't even have to see people to get his job done means that his job, like many others, is being set up to join what is called the "virtual office." His work, like that of the reporters, can be done anywhere and at any time of day, in effect speeding up reporting time and cutting down on office space. Still, for George all this speeding up and cutting out means that editors and reporters have less time to research stories and less of a say in finishing them off. In effect he is now part of a process that produces a standardized, tabloid-style product that differs markedly from the newspaper before the takeover, but looks a lot like other newspapers around the world.

Specialists in office system design, like systems analysts and researchers, argue that systems that don't support the way the work is done are examples of poor system design. Certainly the limited voice-mail operation and the design of a "one size fits all" computer system that ignores the editorial process are examples of this. Yet, as we will see, this type of "poor" technical design is often chosen over other ways of designing systems not out of stupidity or bad management—as systems analysts tend to think—but because it meets cost-cutting objectives and helps control costs by controlling the workers caught up in its web.

Changes in work and office technology don't always have as high a profile as the takeover at George's newspaper. Reengineering takes many shapes, often beginning with the redesign of a job so that pieces of it can be done faster and more cheaply. George's work is an example of a professional job that senior-level managers classify as being difficult to cut into pieces, although we will see that there are other editorial jobs where this has been done. Sheila's work, described in the next story is, on the other hand, more typical of the type of "back-office" job that has over the last decade become both more routinized and less in demand. Here is what happened in the word-processing center where Sheila worked.

Sheila started as a Wang operator in 1980. When I interviewed her in late 1993, the law firm she then worked for, which had over 100 attorneys, was about to merge with a larger firm. As part of the merger plan, arrangements were being made to phase out the old Wang system and transfer everything over to a networked PC-based word-processing system.

Sheila sits in her own enclosed office and supervises an operation that runs twenty-four hours a day, seven days a week, and is staffed by fifteen operators, all of whom are temporary workers. "More attorneys are doing their own word-processing now, but the complicated documents and the long ones still come down here," she says. "The operators have to be highly skilled. They are using two different systems [Wangs and PCs], and the attorneys

A data-entry pool, early 1980s. This type of cubicle set-up, where the height of the walls and the distance from the windows denotes the rank of an employee, is still standard in many corporate offices. [Steelcase]

expect documents in 'perfect' form or else they'll say 'My secretary can do it better than that.'"

Sheila's operation includes document-scanners and fax machines. Behind her office is a large temperature-controlled equipment room for the huge Wang storage files and the computer system. Her work involves much more technical trouble-shooting than it used to. And there is more sharing of documents among attorneys, both within the firm and because of the merger, which has meant that they are now using more complicated software. As part of the merger plan, the word-processing center is being restructured as a document-processing center.

When I left her operation, it was mid-evening and a new shift was coming on. Sheila said she didn't believe that word-processing pools in law firms would fade away, even though there are fewer and fewer private secretaries and more and more computers for the attorneys and paralegals. "Word-processing centers are not as big as they used to be," she stressed, "but they are the focal point for large documents, spillover work, and rush jobs."

By 1995, Sheila was no longer employed at the law firm. As a result of the merger, she was replaced by the supervisor from the other firm. While Sheila had a wide range of technical skills, she was viewed as the "Wang" expert, and the old Wangs were replaced by PCs. Other changes took place as well. Upstairs in the "front" offices of the attorneys, computers now sit on every desk. All the lawyers have been trained in Windows-based Word-Perfect software and are expected to do almost all of their own document processing. Secretaries have been "tripled up," and those who remain handle billing, timesheets, and some letters. The document-processing center is still used for spillover work, as Sheila predicted, but most of it is done at night and on weekends. All of the workers are part-time word-processors who have been sent over by temporary agencies. Word-processing, which was a new job area less than two decades ago, was segregated as a separate piece of office work, only to fall under the ax by firms looking to cut costs.

THE AGE OF INSECURITY

In the 1960s, the United States moved from being classified as an industrial economy, one where the majority of jobs are in factories, to becoming a post-industrial economy based on service and office work. Today over 70 percent of the workforce is in the service sector, with more than 56 million people, or about 46 percent, in office-related jobs, which include managerial, professional, technical, and administrative-support categories.[2] Administrative support, including clerical work (with over 18 million workers), is the largest occupational category—larger even than sales or factory work—yet it has begun to lose formerly dependable jobs like secretaries and bank tellers. Indeed, the growth of all office jobs has slowed down, while jobs in services and sales, with lower wages and more part-time slots, have picked up. The late twentieth century was to be the age of white-collar work—of jobs that were dependable, well paid, clean, and in nice workplaces. But the age of large, centralized offices, with traditional, well-defined jobs, is going to be far shorter than the industrial era that preceded it. More and more office jobs are being spread out over time and space, as the work is done at all times of the night and day by part-time and temporary workers.

For many people, the slowing down and restructuring of office work means less stability and security. Government and business reports tell us that we can expect to switch jobs and careers at least five times in our working lives. But this is the longer term economic view. In everyday life it means that people already employed need to keep an eye out for the next job, while those trying to win a toehold in the office world need to compete with a growing number of people, many of whom have more skills.

After some time, Sheila got a job as a night-shift supervisor in another law firm, making less than she did before. Roger, on the other hand, as a temporary worker for an insurance company, started with fewer skills and less security than Sheila. While he could get by on his salary as a temp, the insurance company he worked for found it could get by without him. The firm, like others in the insurance field, ordered a new computer system that was designed to replace the back-office clerical work of assembling policies. Here is how it happened from Roger's perspective.

Roger, a former insurance-policy assembler,[3] describes his entry into the back office. "For me, [the computer system's arrival] in St. Paul was heralded with a job fair in early 1991. It was a 'casting call' for people with clerical skills and career motivation. Nearly 500 applicants showed up for full-time policy assembly, data-entry and clerical jobs." But, Roger continues, "by the following summer, what had been called 'career opportunities' were disappearing. In one division, eighteen full-time assemblers had been cut to six. The rest of us were temps. It was not a happy place."

"In St. Paul, a good temp wage is $7 an hour. No benefits, of course. The standard work week, 38 hours and 45 minutes, yields a paycheck of $211.75 after deductions, or just under $850 a month if you are never ill ..."

Roger was employed during the time when the new system was being phased in and more than 100 people, taking up a whole floor of an office building were let go, signalling to him that "the job of policy assembly went the way of the buggy whip."

Outside of enjoying the daily banter with his co-workers, this was never what he would call a "great job." Yet its demise has implications for other workers on the bottom rungs of office work. Roger explains it this way:

"Policy assembly is the traditional entry-level job in service-center work. Some underwriters began here. With this job vanishing, the entry-level stakes move higher: when the data-entry job vanishes with the advent of the 'paperless office,' the first rung on the employment ladder will be out of reach for many traditional beginning workers. And the heap of dislocated workers will become bigger."

From the insurance company's perspective, the new computer system was a rational step in integrating the handling of policies, cutting down paperwork and speeding up processing. Indeed, when it was designing and installing the system, the company broke all work tasks down into what they called "work units" and estimated that by the end of the phase-in period, the decrease in the number of work units would have cut costs in half. Office automation in the insurance field has been around since the early days of large mainframe computers, but, as we will see in the coming chapters, it took the better part of the last thirty years for companies like those in insurance to learn enough about the work flow to be able to cut it up into individual steps and then integrate the steps into software programs.

Meanwhile, the automation of clerical work in front offices has followed a different pattern, but the result, when combined with management reorganization and job redesign, has also been heightened insecurity. Secretarial jobs, for example, have been declining as former clerical functions are pushed up onto the desks of professionals and managers. In some cases former secretaries have been able to grab onto some of the newer positions as administrative and executive assistants. But even from this vantage point there are problems. Here is how it looks for Glenda.

Glenda is an executive assistant. She sits in a tiny half-glass partitioned cubicle. "I don't type, file, or answer the phone," she says proudly. "I love voice mail because it freed me from having to be chained to my desk." Glenda works for a large telecommunications company where job titles have been collapsed into four levels. The next rung above her, the "members of technical staff" (who make up most of the office), do all their own word-processing, answer their own phones, and use voice mail and email for their messages. Even the two levels above them, the directors and vice-presidents, generally handle their own calls, although they can switch a call to an executive assistant if they are going to be out.

Glenda describes her job as that of "a buffer, someone who helps things run smoothly." She had worked as an executive secretary for a computer company, but she likes this job much better. "If people need conference rooms, moving requests, or travel reservations, they email me and I get it done for them. We have 'responsibility codes,' and depending on what code you are, you can order things and get budget approval." She is paid comparatively well (she has worked her way up to the low-$30,000s) and enjoys the people she works with. Although she likes it when people come by and "make personal contact," she would rather they send requests by email so that she can have a written record of what they want. A problem she sees, in addition to the lack of office space, is that "over email you can't see a person's facial expression, so sometimes 'flames' start wars when people respond the wrong way to sarcasm or what was meant to be a joke."

Glenda loves her work and the fact that email and voice mail have freed her from the telephone, but the large company she works for doesn't have many people in her position. There is currently about one executive assistant for every 18-20 professional workers, and about half of the assistants are sent over from temporary agencies. Below Glenda's position, almost all support services, from the copy shop through the mailroom, are done by temporary workers. The telecommunications company is just now going through another round of "downsizing" and reorganization, geared, according to articles in the business press, to further reengineer the work flow so that the company can compete in new "telecommunications markets." There is much discussion, over email as well as in the corridors, about who and what jobs will go next.

This telecommunications company, like Roger's insurance firm, is following a pattern where fewer people are doing more work, usually because several tasks, and sometimes several jobs, have been combined into one. This has become possible with the development of voice mail, email, and computer systems that are put in place in order to combine and integrate jobs, and because of management-sponsored work reorganization, including collapsed job ladders and job redesign, resulting in "everything rolled-into-one" jobs.

Feelings of insecurity can come from many places. Certainly lost jobs are part of the problem. But so is the increase in part-time and temporary work. According to official government statistics, in the Spring of 1995 there were more than 4.5 million people working part-time for economic reasons, essentially because they couldn't find full-time work.[4] As part and parcel of Reengineering, management consultants recommend using outsourcing to shrink the workforce (see box on Office Speak for definitions of these terms), spinning parts of companies off into separate units or turning former workers into independent consultants and freelancers. It is now generally estimated that between 25 and 30 percent of the workforce is in some sort of "contingency" status, meaning that these workers have limited or no contractual agreements with their employers. Many work from home and a growing number say that they are trying to start their own businesses.[5]

The way work has been restructured is cloaked in neutral language that makes it sound as if whatever happens is necessary and even inevitable. The often-repeated zippy-sounding phrases also put workers on the defensive when they try to object. The box on the next page gives some key phrases of current "office speak."

THE FREELANCING OF AMERICA

The old contract between employer and employee, which came into being at the start of the industrial period, moved the workplace out of the home, collecting workers under one roof—the factory—and setting a fixed time period for labor. This contract, or set of expectations, was carried over into the early post-industrial period and shaped office work as it developed in the twentieth century. But in the 1990s, as jobs are becoming more and more temporary in nature and the traditional bonds between employer and employee are being cut, increasing numbers of workers are being turned into freelancers. This is almost a return to the not-so-romantic days of medieval Europe, where each freelancer had to swear his allegiance to a lord in exchange for some form of temporary security.

Some freelance work is done as "moonlighting" or second jobs. The Labor Department estimates that about 7.5 million people,

---

Office Speak

Business Process Reengineering (BPR) Often referred to simply as "reengineering." BPR appeared in 1990 and has been called the "hottest management concept since the quality movement" (the hot topic of the 1980s).[6] According to Michael Hammer, the acknowledged coiner of the phrase, this is a chance to "stop paving the cow paths. Instead of embedding outdated processes in silicon and software, we should *obliterate* them and start over."[7]

Downsize To cut costs—usually people—from large organizations. This word, like reengineering, became common in the early 1990s. Laid-off workers soon learned that it was just another way of saying "You're fired." Some companies have begun to use the term "rightsized" in order to get around the deservedly bad reputation of "downsize."

Freelance According to the dictionary, this word appeared in the nineteenth century and referred to mercenary soldiers who offered their services to any "state, party, or cause."[8] Now it generally refers to people who have been "downsized" or "outsourced" (see below) and thus have to sell their services to an organization or customer.

Outsource To cut tasks, jobs, and people from larger organizations and send the work out to smaller firms and individuals, either at home or abroad. Outsourcing became significant in the 1980s and is still occurring at a rapid clip.

Retool In the days of the industrial factory, this term meant scrapping old machines and tools and bringing in new ones. Now it refers to redesigning whole systems, including people, and is generally a clue that massive job changes are underway that will call for big doses of retraining (as in, "These workers need to be 'retooled'"!).

---

or 6 percent of the workforce, does this,[9] but anecdotal evidence points to the fact that many more people than this are working second and third jobs, particularly parents who are trying to keep up with rising costs. A common characteristic of much freelance work is that it has been carved out of the pieces that used to be done by full-time workers. Judith is an intermediate school teacher who has been pulling in textbook writing assignments in the summer in order to help pay for her sons' college expenses.

Judith sits in her basement. The light from her computer screen and a goose-neck reading lamp shine harshly on the piles of paper around her. Working on a piecework contract basis, she writes workbook assignments for elementary school reading textbooks. "You never see the whole picture," she says, going on to explain that "there seems to be no rhyme or reason for what they dole out. Sometimes I get sent Chapter 20 and then Chapter 16. Everything has been pieceworked."

On her last assignment, Judith worked for an editor who was herself under contract to a development house—which was in turn working on "spec" for a publisher. The editor sent Judith work by Federal Express and she FedExed the completed assignment back on a disk. Judith never met the editor; nor did she know what book series the development house was bidding on.

She and her husband used some of the freelance money she earned two years ago to redo their basement and buy a new computer. "It's been paying off," she says, and she was once able to knock off a $2,000 assignment in two weeks by working eighteen hours a day. "But," she continues, "this cut-and-dried textbook writing is drying up as publishers and development houses cut back" because schools are cutting down on their textbook orders.

Judith's friend Pauline has depended on freelance assignments since losing her job when the large textbook publisher she worked for "downsized" ten years ago. The drying up of textbook writing has left her searching for other writing assignments. "There are a lot of other freelancers out there now," she notes, and the competition is fierce. One of her chief problems is that while she sometimes bills $2,000 a month, there are many months with little coming in and too many times when publishers or subcontract agencies tell her "the check is in the mail." Last year she earned only $14,500, not enough to cover her medical costs or pay for car insurance.

Judith's and Pauline's work falls into the Professional category. It requires a good deal of independent decision-making and solid skills in writing as well as familiarity with education and publishing. Yet jobs like these are showing wear and tear as they are divided up into work-unit-like chunks and parcelled out to people who, like temporary workers in clerical jobs, work without benefits and without knowing where the next paycheck is coming from.

In addition, work done at home, the way these jobs are, has taken on many of the isolating and alienating characteristics of work that is done without seeing or coming into contact with other people. Traditional office jobs, like George's and Glenda's, have also been restructured to rely less and less on personal contact and more on the flickering screens of computer systems and the beeping tones of voice mail.

Computer system designers don't emphasize the isolating characteristics, focusing instead on the development of CD-ROM videos, access to remote data bases, and standardization of network links that they say make work more flexible. Software firms foresee profits in these areas.[10] And management experts are generally pleased with these developments because they fit in with plans for further redesigning work so that still more of it can be downsized and outsourced, eventually becoming part of the "virtual office." Yet the blending of workspace and homespace implied by the flexibility of virtual offices brings about a new set of problems.

The following account, adapted from a *New York Times* article,[11] reports on a development that would have been quite unusual a few years ago.

Peggy spends a lot of time on the phone in her car. As an advertising executive, she is one of about forty employees in her company who have been shifted to the "virtual office." The new corporate headquarters is being renovated into "non-territorial offices," places where an ad executive can check in and be temporarily assigned a workspace. Peggy jokes that "we are going from cubes to cubbies," because the space in the new office will be more like a library carrel or a booth in an airport executive lounge than an office cubicle.

Peggy, with Powerbook, modem, portable phone, and email, is a telecommuter. Whether in her home, the front seat of her car, an airport terminal, or a client's office, she can send in her work, check for messages, and look at client data on her computer.

Many management proponents of telecommuting and virtual offices claim that professional workers gain a lot from the arrangement. Peggy is not so sure: it seems to her that her work is expanding to fill all her working hours. Picking up her daughter from nursery school, running household errands, and finding a quiet place to do creative work all vie for her time. As she puts it, "I have the feeling that it is no longer my life fitting into my work, but my work fitting into my life."

THINGS ARE NOT ALWAYS WHAT THEY SEEM

Magazines and radio and TV talk shows make it sound as if high-tech jobs are cutting a path to a high-skill, high-wage future. But, as the analysis in this book will show, there is little evidence from government statistics, business surveys, or anecdotal accounts to support this. Like Alice in the strange landscape of the *Looking Glass*, we also find ourselves in need of a map to show us where we have been and help us figure out where we want to go. When you read magazines or listen to talk shows, you might think that it is technology alone that has the majority of office workers spending their days peering at computer screens in their roles as finder, assemblers, and keepers of information. In the 1970s, social scientist Daniel Bell was one of the first to write about an "information society,"[12] while the term "knowledge worker" came into use in the 1980s. Like the popular press, social scientists and other academics have for the most part jumped on the "information society" bandwagon, in effect keeping alive the assumption that somehow technology advances, and that this is automatically good for everybody.

But the idea that technology advances makes technology sound like the chess pieces that move themselves in *Alice in Wonderland*. To understand what is happening today, we need to move beyond make-believe and take a clear look around. Whatever technological "advancement" is, it is a rocky road when seen through the eyes of the workers and managers caught in the process.

Unfortunately, the glowing language of "advancement" has kept us from looking closely at the changes that are taking place in the workplace, and at how technology has been designed to support these changes. If you look around, you can easily find many people you know who have stories to tell about how their work has changed or is changing. Some of the things people talk about concern new office systems, but many others focus on work reorganization, company policies, and issues of job security. Ten years ago, most office workers had fairly well-defined occupational titles and worked in more-or-less traditional office settings. Today, people who enter the labor market, as well as those already in it, are finding themselves with brand-new job titles (or even in jobs without a title) and in a wide variety of workplaces, not just office cubicles.

Two economic issues have become strikingly clear. The first deals with the restructuring of the *labor market*, where people compete for jobs and hope they have the right skills and experi-

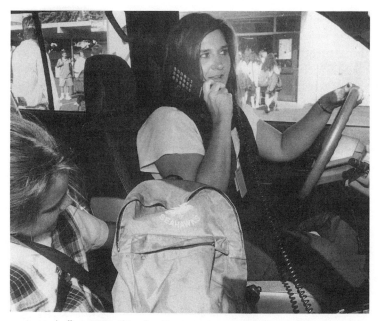

A virtual office, 1993. This advertising executive, a telecommuter, checks her next appointment while picking her daughter up from school. [Bart Bartholomew/NYT Pictures]

ence. As corporate or long-term company jobs are dismantled, more people are being pushed into highly competitive labor markets for short-term, temporary, or freelance jobs. This has the effect of keeping salaries and wages down. The second issue concerns the restructuring of the *labor process*, or the way the work is done. More jobs and pieces of jobs have been combined, making work more intensive. And as more office workers need to use computers to get their jobs done, more are expected to have computer skills—which means that managers don't necessarily have to pay them for these skills.

Certainly the introduction of office technology has had an important role in bringing about both forms of restructuring. There is no question that the falling prices of all kinds of office technology, including computers, fax machines, voice mail, telephone systems, and copiers, coupled with standardization and the availability of less expensive software, has made it easier for management to justify introducing new office systems. But stories of workplace change need to be told in context, and the context includes not just the technology but also the reasons for its use. The restructuring of work that has occurred did not come about overnight; nor did it come about by whim or accident.

This book tells the story of changes in office work from the 1950s through the mid-1990s. It focuses on the way work has been structured in each period, and the ways that technology has been shaped in order to bring this structuring about. None of the developments, in and of themselves, are inevitable. Further, what is good for an individual company is not necessarily good for the workers in that company or for the larger economy and society.

The next chapter looks at developments in office work in the 1950s and 1960s, highlighting the rise of multinational corporations and how corporate life then shaped office work. It uses two seemingly different occupations, secretaries and computer programmers, to illustrate how work was divided and office automation was first applied to the back-office part.

Chapter 3 looks at office work and technology in the 1970s. During that period, offices were patterned after factories, and management theory pushed for jobs with an increased number of routine and repetitive functions. Computer systems were made to fit this pattern.

Chapter 4 focuses on the 1980s, a period of flux and contradiction for the organization of office work and the technology used to support it. The decade opened with much talk of the "office of the future" and the "paperless office," but it wasn't until mid-decade that personal computers and fax machines became common, and it wasn't until the end of the decade that voice mail and networks made it possible to scatter office work—to create the "virtual office" of the 1990s. Management theory and practice

were almost equally divided during this period between continuing the routinization of work so common in the 1960s and 1970s
and integrating and combining functions into new job categories.
Sometimes, management plans for greater efficiency and office
automation didn't fit together. In the 1950s and 1960s, for example, making office work fit a factory assembly-line model made
it take longer to get some things done and resulted in clumsy
computer systems. In the 1980s, office systems were supposed to
bring about a paperless office, but by all accounts more and more
paperwork was created.[13] The rocky road of technical change is
littered with proposals that highlight contradictions and clashes
between management plans and workplace practice.

The 1990s, the subject of Chapters 5 and 6, are like a braid
weaving together the developments that began in the earlier
periods. Work that had already been routinized could now be
outsourced and spread among "virtual offices." And newly integrated forms of work have led to fewer people working longer
hours or more intensely, doing work that had previously been
done by more people. Routinized work, often called "deskilled"
work, and integrated work, referred to as "upskilled" or
"reskilled" work, are two pieces of the same pattern: according to
management theory, tasks can only be integrated after routine
functions have been identified and sorted out.

Chapter 7 closes with an analysis of all these developments and
looks at change as a process—a process that can be influenced.
Office technology—computers, copiers, fax machines, voice
mail, and the like—is created by people. It is a social invention:
the hardware and the software are created by people, and they are
used, changed, and reused by people. If this book were a murder
mystery, we would discover that it wasn't technology that "did
it," but the people who make the decisions about what technology
is designed for and how it is used. The next chapter sets the stage
for this story.

2

THE 1950s AND 1960s: DAWN OF THE COMPUTER AGE

In the enormous file of the office, in all the calculating rooms, accountants and purchasing agents replace the man who did his own figuring. And in the lower reaches of the white-collar world, office operatives grind along, loading and emptying the filing system; there are private secretaries and typists, entry clerks, billing clerks, corresponding clerks—a thousand kinds of clerks; the operators of light machinery, comptometers, dictaphones, addressographs; and the receptionists to let you in or keep you out.
—C. Wright Mills, *White Collar*, 1951[1]

Most of the lower income white-collar jobs that sociologist C. Wright Mills described in his classic book *White Collar* are gone now, or are done in totally different ways. Yet his description of the "enormous file of the office" sets the stage for understanding the beginning of what came to be known, among social scientists and the media, as the "computer and information age." This period, which began after World War II, has also been given a string of titles that refer to its apparently "revolutionary" nature, hinting that the computer, information, and organizational "revolutions" would bring us into a new era of easier living and better jobs.

This optimism rested on two pillars of change after World War II: the global expansion of businesses, which created the need for more information in the form of documents to record transactions; and the growing reliance on office technology to support these new functions. The first resulted in an increase in the number of office workers needed to operate the new machines and handle all the documents. The second, the growing reliance on office technology, initially supported the clerical and operator jobs that Mills described but later led to enormous changes in their numbers and function.

WHAT'S GOOD FOR THE COUNTRY?

"What is good for General Motors is good for the country."
—Charles Wilson, Secretary of Defense
under Dwight D. Eisenhower

As a child growing up in the 1950s, I learned that the United States was the "best of all possible places." We were taught to expect continued economic growth, more and more jobs, growing prosperity, and a better standard of living, all of which were to be brought to us by companies like General Electric, which, as its advertising put it, "brought good things to life." But the world was not always like a scene from the TV sitcom "Father Knows Best." I remember asking a lot of questions during the recession of 1957-1958, when the news shows were telling us that the recession was caused by "people not buying enough." If we would only go out and buy more cars and home appliances, the economy would get back on track—or so we were told. But it didn't make sense to me that it was the fault of us, the consumers, that the economy wasn't growing. Nor did it make sense that the General Motors plant down the road from my father's hardware store had laid off thousands of workers who certainly couldn't be better consumers if they weren't getting paid. To my young eyes, what was merely a problem for General Motors, or General Electric, or any of the other big companies, was a disaster for the people who worked for them. And so in the 1960s I went to college to study economics, only to find that mainstream economists propagated this same belief in the ability of companies to create job growth and higher a standard of living for all.

It is true that in the 1950s and 1960s, the number of steady jobs *was* increasing, productivity was up, and the economy, despite a few recessions along the way, *was* growing. But this growth was not the result of individual companies "doing the right thing"; rather, it was based primarily on the economic and military dominance that the United States had won for itself following the destruction of the other big economies in World War II. U.S. companies were in a sense the "only game in town," the only companies able to meet the growing worldwide demand for goods and services.

The language and ideology of global competition and increased productivity that we hear today is almost a rerun (with some new words thrown in) of what I heard in the 1950s. Today we are told that it is our fault as consumers if we don't buy enough to keep the economy rolling (in other words, that we don't create enough demand), and that it is our fault that we aren't more productive so that we can help U.S. companies compete in the heated-up global marketplace (in other words, that we don't create enough supply). Since factory work has already been pressed into more flexible production through the use of robots and by reorganizing the work,[2] the emphasis has shifted to making middle-class white-collar workers, who came into prominence in the 1950s, just as flexible.

A secretarial pool, late 1940s. Secretarial work offered employment of a higher status than the factory or servant work that had been available to women a generation earlier. [Culver Pictures]

WHITE–COLLAR WORKERS ARRIVE

According to C. Wright Mills, "In the early nineteenth century, although there are no exact figures, probably four-fifths of the occupied population were self-employed enterprisers. By 1870, only about one-third, and by 1940, only about one-fifth, were still in the 'old' middle class."[3] These small entrepreneurs—shop owners, small-business owners, merchants, traders, and small farmers—had accumulated enough money to own independent property and thus earn their own living. But by the end of the nineteenth century, many businesses were big enough and strong enough to begin to buy out smaller and weaker companies, beginning the march toward monopolies and large industrial holdings. By the 1950s, the United States had been transformed from a nation of small farmers and entrepreneurs into a nation of employees. One group of these new employees was made up of "white-collar workers," who were becoming the backbone of a "new" middle class.

In the years after World War II, white-collar work was seen as a ticket to upward mobility. Housing prices were comparatively low and a great deal of affordable housing was being built for returning soldiers. Support for the housing boom came, in part, from the government's policy of ensuring low-cost mortgages (around 4 percent) to potential home buyers. At the same time, low-cost loans for GIs to go to college meant that there was a growing number of better educated men who formed a ready pool of white-collar labor. The new middle class owned property, but not the kind or amount that would make them into entrepreneurs or people owning their own businesses. Thus the "American Dream" shifted. Owning homes and cars replaced owning shops, businesses, and the means of production (property and tools controlled by an owner). In essence, the entrepreneurial culture of the last century was replaced by a new corporate one.

The growing prominence of corporations was one cornerstone of this period. Working as a salaried white-collar employee for "the organization" provided solid benefits, prestige, security, and the opportunity for promotion. Corporate life, while bureaucratic and regimented, provided a career, not just a job. That is, it did this for those who fit the model of the newly emerging corporate world—people who, prior to the civil rights movement of the 1950s and 1960s and the women's movement of the 1970s and 1980s, were primarily white college-educated men. Indeed, government policy and social pressure following World War II were set up to push women out of the labor force.[4] But in the 1950s, 1960s, and early 1970s, the demand for white-collar workers was generally greater than the supply of people coming into the labor market. So a small but significant number of educated and trained women were accepted into clerical, administrative, and some professional positions in this period.

Corporate and business expansion was fueled by the growth of huge government-sponsored programs to mass-produce weapons and supplies for the military. It was also sparked by large organizations taking advantage of U.S. military supremacy in much of the non-Communist world to expand their businesses into third world countries, where they were able to win access to cheap resources and cheaper labor. Defense Secretary Charles Wilson was half right—U.S. military and political power was good for General Motors, and for General Electric, General Mills, and the generals, both private and public, who profited from international expansion.

The new multinational trade expansion was founded on corporate rules and practices that were based on standardization, routinization, and belief in bureaucratic policy. Bureaucracy was not new. It had been seen in military form in the last century and was analyzed and critiqued by the German sociologist Max · Weber back at the turn of this century. Centralization of administration and control of operations was a first principle of bureaucracy. This type of centralized administration was backed by hierarchical rules and carried out using an intensive division of labor and standardization of tasks. Large national and multinational corporations applied these ideas to white-collar work, showing that office tasks could be divided and thus, like factory tasks, become more easily controlled. In the 1950s, bureaucratic principles and practices were applied on an international scale.

For the most part, the popular press portrayed bureaucratic corporate life as part and parcel of "getting a good job." Yet the dark side of life in an organization was visible as well. Novels like *The Man in the Gray Flannel Suit*, and studies like William Whyte's *The Organization Man*, addressed the problems of conformity and stress. The "organization man" (and he was a man) came to typify the period of corporate expansion. As we will see in the following examples, this period was one where the foundations of divided and controlled work were established inside office walls. At the same time that front-office, sometimes prestigious, jobs were made to appear to be personifications of corporate life, many tasks were being divided and separated out into lower paid, back-office functions. The "divide-and-conquer" approach made few distinctions between the established area of clerical work and the newly minted field of computer programming.

DIVIDING FRONT FROM BACK OFFICES

By the 1950s secretarial and clerical work was a well accepted field for women. But it wasn't always that way. Before the 1880s, clerical work was done by men, who were viewed by owners and managers as possible recruits into the business.

Oddly enough, the "feminization" of clerical work had something to do with the introduction of machinery, in this case typewriters. In 1874 Remington, a manufacturer of guns, began to mass produce "type writers." Since typewriting as a job was too new to have any particular association with men or women, the use of female "type-writers"—as the occupation was first called—was not perceived as a threat to male secretaries. In this way, the use of the keyboard, and indeed the use of office equipment in general, became associated with women's work.

But it was also the growth of the field that gave women a chance to step "up" to office work. At the turn of the century, as business and the associated paperwork expanded, there was a growing demand for clerical workers, and at the same time there were more educated women who needed to work. These two trends together created an opening for women who had previously only had the choice of factory work or servant positions.[5] After World War II, and especially in the 1950s, when women working in male-defined positions were stigmatized socially, they were allowed to stay in the comparatively lower paid secretarial and clerical areas. This was in part because their use of typewriters,

A SHORT SOCIAL HISTORY OF SECRETARIAL WORK[6]

- **1873** When the YWCA trains eight women to work on typewriters, doctors are asked to certify that the women are physically and mentally strong enough to do the job.

- **1875** A want ad for female typists appears in a New York newspaper. It reads: "Mere girls are now earning from $10 to $20 a week with the 'Type-Writer.'"

- **1900** According to the Census Bureau, there are more than 100,000 people working as secretaries, stenographers, and typists.

- **1911** The Katharine Gibbs secretarial school is founded. It not only teaches typewriting and office skills, but specializes in teaching proper behavior and dress. White gloves are its graduates' trademark.

- **1920** There are more than 1 million women clerical workers.

- **1950** From this point on, a secretary is as least as likely to be married as single.

- **1960** Of the more than 1.4 million secretaries in the United States, only 42,000 (or 2.9 percent) are men.

stenographic equipment, and adding machines was already accepted. Such work provided opportunities for women from a range of ethnic and racial backgrounds, as well as acceptable openings for both older and married women. Meanwhile, the positions that some women had formerly held, such as supervisory jobs, were becoming part of a new corporate executive career track—the twentieth century way to recruit men into the business world.

Despite its low pay, office work was viewed as relatively safe, clean, and of higher status than factory or domestic work. More than a hundred years ago, in 1890, female typists earned 1.8 times more than women factory workers, but by the 1950s routine clerical jobs paid less than factory jobs: the status and security of the work were more attractive than the pay.[7]

The word secretary originally came from the word "secret"—"one entrusted with secrets." In other words, a secretary was to be someone who could act as a gatekeeper, guarding the secrets of the boss and carrying out a wide range of decisions and tasks that were often invisible to him.[8] Clerical work, an even broader category, began to be carved out of secretarial functions in the early part of the twentieth century, and by the 1950s included typists, file clerks, and large numbers of people doing the behind-the-scenes work of keeping documents and papers in order—carrying out what managers saw as the housework of the office.

The *visible* parts of secretarial work, like typing and filing, have increasingly been separated, routinized, and automated, while the more *invisible* tasks, such as gatekeeping, as well as prioritizing the boss's work, scheduling, and making the office run smoothly, have resisted—at least until recently—such routinization and automation. Managers and efficiency experts (the forerunners of today's management consultants) made the visible tasks into back-office functions, while the harder to quantify and therefore more difficult to routinize secretarial work stayed in the front office.

In the 1950s, this splitting of back- from front-office functions was also a dividing line between mechanized functions and those that used very little in the way of equipment. Until the widespread use of the word-processor, for example, secretaries used typewriters, dictaphones, and telephones, while the machines for calculating, copying, addressing, and performing other specialized functions were put where those entering the office would not see them.

This type of division of routine from nonroutine tasks followed management objectives for increasing productivity and control over the growing clerical workforce. The routine work being done in the back office took many forms: there were bank check processors working with MICR (magnetic ink character recognition) machines, keypunch operators and verifiers, duplicating-machine operators, mainframe computer operators in glassed-in "operations rooms," and of course typists. The split in pay scales and working environments was a concrete reminder of the physical separation of front- and back-office functions.

In the 1960s, upper management pushed for, and got, separate typing pools—areas (usually in the basement or some other out-of-the-way place) where work could be "sent down" to typists whose sole function was to type and send the finished product "back up." Many managers at first did not like this breakdown in what Barbara Garson, in a book called *The Electronic Sweatshop*, has called "office monogamy"—the one boss–one secretary relationship—but management experts argued that it was much more efficient.[9] Typing pools, which were much later to become word-processing centers, were the result of a division of labor that classified typing as "hands" work and managerial and professional duties as "head" work—a crucial division that we will hear more about in the next chapter. This division has been debated, and evaluated, for the past thirty years, but it is still around. Many of the people who are caught up in it argue that it often results in sending the same work "down" to the pool again and again because the division causes communication breakdowns. Juliet Webster, a sociologist who has studied clerical work, describes one group of British typists, who when dictation tapes were sent to them acted out their frustration this way:

> If they said "er," we put "er" in.... So some of them came back and were furious about this and said, "This is absolute rubbish." We said, "Well, that is what you dictated, so we typed it." They wouldn't admit that they had done it.... And they do. They are really bad. They say "Oh no, typist," so we typed "Oh no, typist." They didn't like that at all.[10]

Today the argument is made that centralized "pools" are not very effective, in part because it has been acknowledged that dividing the work this way interferes with people talking to each other in order to get things done, and in part because this division ignores "invisible" or tacit skills, just as these British typists pointed out. But during the heyday of pools—the 1960s, 1970s, and most of the 1980s—they created the framework for routinizing many tasks, such as form letters and data-entry work. And, not incidentally, the pool and back-office form of work organization played a major role in the way new office equipment was designed, because it reinforced management's belief that work needed to be divided and routinized *before* new technology could be effectively introduced.

SLICING COMPUTER OPERATIONS FROM PROGRAMMING

In the 1950s computer programming was a brand-new field, touted as the up-and-coming occupation and stereotyped as a "man's occupation," yet it had not started out that way. During World War II, when the first experimental computer (called the ENIAC) was developed, women were employed as "computers," a new occupation established to do what we now call programming. The recruitment of men into the field started as computer manufacturers and large companies, lacking a large enough pool of already trained applicants and faced with the fact that after the war women were being encouraged to leave professional jobs, lured mathematicians by offering them high pay and a great deal of job freedom. But this phase only lasted from the mid-1950s through the mid-1960s. After that, the demand for programmers and the paucity of workers with a science education (computer science programs did not appear until the late 1960s) meant that the math—and therefore presumably male-oriented—qualifications were often ignored. In fact, during the Vietnam war, when men were in relatively short supply in the labor market, women began to enter the field in small but noticeable numbers. And the need for math and science qualifications proved essential only for the comparatively small handful of programmers who worked on scientific systems. By the 1960s the bulk of the computer industry

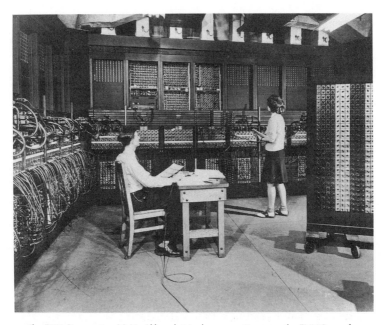

The ENIAC computer, 1946. Although it took up an entire room, the ENIAC was far slower and had a fraction of the storage capacity of today's desktop PC. Note the woman "computer." [IBM Archives]

was moving in the direction of business-oriented applications, although it remained a field that was overwhelmingly male.

The history of computer work doesn't necessarily parallel the clerical field, but there are some interesting similarities in the way computer operations was separated from programming and made into a back-office function. With programming as with clerical work, this division of labor, which later extended to other programming functions, was aimed at cutting labor costs and managing workers more closely.

In the 1960s, as the demand for programmers grew, programmers had their choice of jobs, leaving managers to complain about the programmers' free-wheeling, independent spirit.[11] In fact, many early programmers saw themselves as independent craftspeople, much like the image of the computer "hacker" today. An English sociologist described how the culture of the early programmers collided with the corporate culture:

> In fact, their strange work time-table and casual dress attracted criticism. The programmers also disrupted company rules about clocking on and off. This, together with the reward their market position afforded them at such a comparatively young age, created problems within the company status system.[12]

But it wasn't just their clothing or uncorporate-like behavior that bothered management. These problems were manifestations of the fact that programmers had control over what they did. A computer programmer working in 1977 fondly recalled his job in the preceding era:

> I remember that in the 1950s and early 1960s, I was a "jack of all trades." As a programmer I got to deal with the whole process. I would think through a problem, talk to the clients, write my own code, and operate the machine. I loved it—particularly the chance to see something through from beginning to end.[13]

By the mid-1960s, these "jacks of all trades" didn't fit into the increasingly compartmentalized corporate structure. The first step that management took to gain control over the programming workforce was to divide the conceptual work of programming from the more physical tasks of computer operations. Although this division was put into effect in the aerospace industry in the mid-1950s and subsequently used by companies that had defense contracts, it wasn't until the mid-1960s that it spread elsewhere. By 1965, when IBM began installing the general-purpose System 360, both the more expensive hardware (a large mainframe computer) and the easier to use software (an operating system that could be controlled through commands rather than operators working switches), gave upper and middle managers room to begin enforcing the separation of programming from operations. Operators were to stay in the "machine room" tending the computer, while programmers were to sit upstairs and write the instructions. Those of us in the field at the time remember feeling that a firm division of labor had been introduced almost overnight. It was many years before it was effective, however, because, as with the division between back- and front-office tasks, work did not flow smoothly across the physically divided workforce. Programmers who were used to operating the computer in order to test programs found it difficult to explain, through written instructions, what had to be done. And operators, much like typists in back-office pools, were blamed for mistakes they couldn't even ask questions about. The division between programming and operations further divided workers and sliced up tasks that could, at least theoretically, have been controlled by bureaucratic principles.

ENTERING THE COMPUTER AGE

The 1950s and 1960s were full of enthusiasm for what most observers saw as a revolutionary new era. Information was portrayed as the key to knowledge and power—something that could be available to all. Television, the new magic eye into people's homes, provided advertisers with huge audiences that appeared to be delighted with the advantages of the new technology. And chief among the so-called wonders of the age was the computer.

The first computer was developed to calculate ballistic trajectories for bombing raids at the end of World War II (see the box on the next page). This massive machine, made up of huge vacuum tubes, was seen more as a marvel than as a prototype for a new computer industry. In the early 1950s, a few machines were leased to the government and to large corporations, but they were designed primarily for scientific "number-crunching," and were not viewed as essential for business. Certainly their huge size (taking up 100-foot-long rooms) and comparatively unreliable performance (vacuum tubes, like light bulbs, burn out with use) did not make them seem like the wave of the future.

In 1959, a "second generation" of computers was introduced

A SHORT SOCIAL HISTORY OF COMPUTING

- **1830s** Charles Babbage and Lady Ada Lovelace work on the design for an "analytical" engine that becomes the basis for later computers. Babbage thinks that division of labor and mechanization can be applied to mental as well as manual tasks. He becomes known as the "father" of modern computers; Ada Lovelace, the first programmer, later has the programming language ADA named after her.

- **1890** Herman Hollerith is commissioned to design a system for tabulating the census. He comes up with the 80-column punched card, the basis for the current standard for turning characters and numbers into electronic "bytes" of information. The 80 columns also still serve as the standard for computer screen displays.

- **1944-1945** The first electronic computer, the ENIAC, is a huge room full of vacuum tubes. It is designed to calculate ballistic trajectories for bombs dropped from airplanes. Grace Hopper, a Navy officer, is head of the programming team.

- **1950** Remington Rand, which has moved from guns to typewriters, delivers a UNIVAC computer to the government to use in processing the census.

- **1954** General Electric becomes the first private company to install a computer. It is used for payroll processing.

- **1959** The "second generation" of computers is introduced. They use transistors instead of vacuum tubes and are considerably smaller and faster than their predecessors. COBOL and FORTRAN, easier to use programming languages, come into use.

- **1965** "Third generation" computers, which use integrated circuits, are introduced. Programming for businesses begins to take off.

that used transistors rather than vacuum tubes, making the machines somewhat smaller (they still required huge rooms and power supplies, however) and more reliable. They had the advantage of using programming languages like FORTRAN and COBOL developed for them, making it easier for more people to code programs. They were in turn replaced, after 1965, by the third generation of computers, which used integrated circuits. It was these machines that finally ushered in the more widespread use of mainframe computers and prompted computer manufacturers and corporations to develop standardized software tools to be used with them.

The standardization and division of labor that were the mainstays of corporate organization also provided the principles on which the new computer programs were designed. At first, the software applications developed for these computers were custom designed for each company. They generally replicated well-defined tasks, such as calculating payroll deductions and printing inventory lists. If the tasks and procedures in a particular business or area were not already defined, the systems development process called for standardization before computerization began. In this way company after company developed codes and procedures for making processes like payrolls more routine. Indeed, functions that weren't ripe for routinization didn't fit into the programming mold. The 1957 film *Desk Set* is a good example of what happens when systems analysts tried to routinize work without really understanding it. The film featured a librarian (played by Katherine Hepburn) and a computer efficiency expert (Spencer Tracy) who was hired to automate the library staff. In the end, the computer Tracy installs blows up, unable to keep up with the enormous knowledge and skill that Hepburn and her librarians had been using in their work.

This Hollywood version of the result of installing computers was meant to calm workers' fears about losing jobs through automation. But meanwhile, most companies followed the path of cutting departments and jobs up into smaller pieces and then assigning programmers to write programs for these increasingly standardized tasks, rather than trying to automate entire departments.

This design process, like corporate processes in general, was not without its problems. In 1965, Robert Boguslaw, a systems analyst and critic, attempted to challenge the focus on standardization and routinization. Trying to reach an audience of system developers and managers and referring to computer system developers as the "new utopians," he wrote:

> And so it is that the new utopians retain their aloofness from human and social problems presented by the fact or threat of machined systems and automation. They are concerned with neither souls nor stomachs. People problems are left to the after-the-fact efforts of social scientists.[14]

But such warnings, like warnings about the pernicious effects of the increasing division of labor and misgivings about bureaucratic conformity, went unheeded. Computer applications continued down a path that supported the management objective of dividing labor and lowering costs. In this way, there were programs developed to separate those who keypunched data from those who entered it on forms, to separate customer relations specialists from clerical workers doing the record keeping, and so on.

The 1950s and 1960s were the beginning of the "information age"—the growth of business and government, and the enormous accumulation of paperwork and information to keep them going. In this period, management planning focused primarily on job reorganization and the introduction of isolated pieces of office equipment. In fact, while computers were a much talked about highlight of the period, very little computerization actually took place. Rather, this was a period of preparing for it. But in the next decade, as the volume of work increased and the labor costs, from management's perspective, sky-rocketed, automation came to be considered as applicable to the office as it was the factory.

A computer operations room, late 1960s. Note the two types of storage systems: magnetic tapes processed batch jobs sequentially, while the disk drives (to the right of the operators) were random access—the forerunners of today's diskettes. [IBM Archives]

By 1973, when the U.S. government study called *Work in America* was published, the bubble seemed to have burst on the golden future of automation and work. The report, which included a section entitled "White-Collar Woes," documented that many workers—including professionals, managers, technical workers, and clericals—were dissatisfied with their jobs because pieces of their work had been cut up and put into routine parcels, as if it was factory work. We will now look at how this process, which began in the 1950s and 1960s, accelerated in the 1970s.

3

THE 1970s: THE OFFICE AS THE FACTORY OF THE FUTURE

The office today, where work is segmented and authoritarian, is often a factory. For a growing number of jobs, there is little to distinguish them but the color of the worker's collar: computer keypunch operations and typing pools share much in common with the automobile assembly-line.

—*Work in America*, 1973[1]

While office work in the 1970s looked a lot like office work in the 1960s, there was much going on behind the scenes that would make office work more predictable and therefore easier to code into computer programs. This would not be a simple process. Management theory held that work in the "information age" required a great deal of mental processing, making it difficult to codify and simplify work that was done inside of peoples' heads.

This was a decade of isolating people, tasks, and jobs, essentially separating the "head" of information work from the "hands" of data processing. More and more tasks, particularly those in clerical areas and in back offices, were being treated like manual work. Data processing by definition dealt with information that had been coded and cut up into bits of data. The factory assembly line had accomplished something similar in the early part of the century, when craft workers who used skill and knowledge to make things were replaced by assembly-line workers whose rhythm of work was made more routine and speeded up to fit in with automation.

Here we will first take a look at how office work was done, followed by a description of how and why computer programs were designed to fit this pattern. In the offices of large corporations in the 1970s, closed rooms lined the building's window walls, with an open space in the middle for secretaries and clerical staff. Managers, analysts, and other professionals, depending on their status within the company hierarchy, had the windowed offices. A telephone was usually the only piece of equipment on their desks. In the center, the clerical workers' metal desks marched row on row, lit by the harsh glare of overhead florescent lights. Each of these desks had a protruding "L," where an electric typewriter sat, along with a telephone and maybe some Dictaphone equipment. Most corporate and government front offices looked like this through the early 1980s, and some still do. A good example of how this pre-computer office looked can be seen in the film *9 to 5,* which starred Dolly Parton as a secretary, Lily Tomlin as an office manager, and Jane Fonda as a new assistant.

In the 1970s, there was rarely more than one computer in any organization or, for the larger organizations, in any one division. These mainframe computers were expensive to buy or lease and very costly to maintain. In 1976, for example, a medium-sized computer cost about $360,000 for the hardware alone, while software development costs and operations ran to many times that amount.[2] And this was a machine that had far less storage capacity and was slower than most desktop computers today.

In some offices, mainframes were connected by wires to "dumb terminals," essentially monitors with attached keyboards that had no computing capacity of their own. The use of these terminals for data-entry work followed the pattern established for clerical work in the 1960s: it was treated as routine work, and was, from upper managements' point of view, pushed "out of sight" and almost "out of mind."

The first word-processors were introduced in the 1970s. These "stand-alone" machines were designed to speed up typing and error correction, and also included shortcuts for deleting words and letters and specialized keys for "Saving" and "Printing." They were thus less computers than souped-up typewriters with some electronic functions built in. The people who used them once again were named after the machines—word-processors.

Word-processing machines required new skills and many typists viewed them as a way to upgrade routine work. Some secretaries were able to use their knowledge of word-processing as a stepping stone to better pay, but for clerical workers whose work had already been routinized, word-processing merely replaced the old typing pool. By placing the machines in the back office, management treated the workers who were using them as routine processors, cutting short the possibility of turning word-processing into an upwardly mobile career ladder.

At the same time, insurance-claim processors, credit card clerks, and other back-office workers were moved into their own departments—often deep in the basement of an office building or off in a separate, low-rent building, where they were even more crammed together than workers in front-office clerical areas. The pattern of sending jobs and people off was, from management's perspective, a prerequisite for developing computer programs.

Keypunch operators prepare data cards on the IBM 24 Key Punch. Keypunch machines were used well into the 1970s, even though terminals and word-processing machines had already been introduced. [FPG International]

PROCESSING DATA: THE FACTORY MODEL

During the 1970s, mainframe computers became a fact of organizational life. Most of the "bugs," or programming quirks, in the mainframe operating systems had been ironed out and companies were beginning to develop applications that could handle large volumes of transactions. Insurance companies, banks, airlines, securities firms, and government agencies had high volumes of data and a large amount of repetitive work, characteristics that made them candidates for computer processing. The majority of applications were run as "batches," meaning that masses of data were accumulated and processed at periodic intervals—once a day for a bank, for example, or once a week for a payroll.

Standard bureaucratic management practices were used in supervising the development of software programs to do this work. Systems analysis—the process of designing programs—reflected both its engineering roots in Operations Research during World War II and its managerial antecedents in isolating problems and separating tasks. The emphasis was on managing quantitative information—taking so-called raw data and turning it into numbers that management could review and accountants could record. This was a continuation of the management practices of the 1960s that emphasized standardization—in this case, simplifying and "rationalizing" information into standard chunks of data. The combination of routinizing tasks and standardizing data led to computer systems that recorded only routine transactions, such as accepting or rejecting insurance claims, processing payrolls at regular intervals, and filling flight reservations by destination. This essentially replicated the routine processing done by factory assembly lines.

Critics of what has come to be called the rationalistic version of system development argue that this type of analysis tends to develop computer programs that look at applications only from the perspective of those at the top of the organization. This top-down approach sees organizations as structures that can be formally described, reducing jobs and tasks to simple procedures.[3] In effect, turning work into a step-by-step, linear process forces systems analysts to think in narrow pathways, where the emphasis is on isolating problems and searching for the one "right" solution. In fact, this type of narrow systems thinking was applied to all kinds of issues in the late 1960s and 1970s. In a book entitled *Redesigning the Future: A Systems Approach to Societal Programs*, systems analyst Russell Ackoff spelled out the problems this approach created:

> [Computer systems fail] more often because we solve the wrong problem than because we get the wrong solution to the right problem.... The problems we select for solution and the way we

formulate them depends more on our philosophy and world view than on our science and technology.[4]

Viewed from the perspective of the people who are doing the day-to-day work, computer systems more often than not appear to be solutions to the wrong problems. Looking back, we can see that computer systems that were designed to isolate specific tasks also further isolated and divided labor practices—affecting jobs in more than one isolated area. In social work agencies, for example, computer systems counted welfare recipients and calculated "allowable" sums based on pre-programmed formulae. This type of software moved social work further along a path that divided the work into such steps as "intake" and "maintenance," turning clients into numbers to be processed by the system and taking skill and responsibility away from the social workers—who were reduced to the now-familiar phrase, "I'm sorry, I don't have anything to do with it—the computer did it." As Ackoff pointed out, this type of change wasn't so much a result of technology but of the world view of managers who accepted the systems approach as gospel. In social work, the systems approach brought about lower costs because routine processing meant that fewer social workers could handle the same number of clients, and a larger number of clients could be rejected from the system based on computer codes rather than human judgment.[5]

Many management analysts and consultants still argue that it was the limitations of the technology that produced such repetitive routine processing. This seems doubtful. By emphasizing the hardware and ignoring the human side, they ignore what was really happening. For instance, even though computer terminals were available in the late 1960s, IBM marketed hardware based on keypunch cards into the early 1970s. It claimed that this was because its clients had already invested in keypunch equipment and that applications based on batched keypunch cards were easier to manage. This worked as a marketing strategy, but it also slowed the development of more interactive systems—those that would make it possible to enter and use information at the same time. Similarly, in the early 1970s both GE and RCA tried to get into "time-sharing" software, which would make it possible for many departments and many workers to access information on a mainframe simultaneously.[6] While this was to become the heart of most systems in the late 1970s and early 1980s, it was at first not very successful, in part because managers in large companies and government agencies didn't want to take a chance with something new, and because it didn't fit with established bureaucratic beliefs about who should have access to information. In the early 1970s, both GE and RCA had left the mainframe business, unable to compete with IBM, which was relying on its established customer base and continuing with the standard, and familiar, products. This is one reason why the factory model of automation won out over alternative approaches.

Indeed, contrary to popular stories, saleable new technology is rarely developed in people's garages and basements. Instead, it is the result of long periods of research and development and almost always comes from, or is ordered by, large companies. Sometimes, in fact, the potential of a new technology is not immediately recognized, as the following story, and the box on p. 58 illustrates.

A STORY OF A WRITING TABLET

In the spring of 1968 I was working for IBM as a Programmer Analyst. During a lull between projects, my manager assigned me to take part in a market analysis of a new product and I was sent up to the IBM laboratories in Yorktown, New York, to see a new "writing table." The tablet was the size of a piece of writing paper and about twice as thick as a pad. It could read printing or handwriting, and whatever was written on it was input into a mainframe computer for processing or storage. My assignment was to assess if this type of device would be useful for computer programmers—whether they would want to code their programs on it or continue to send their written code down to the keypunch department (remember this was 1968 and there were as yet no desktop computers). And so I was sent to company offices around the country to interview programmers, managers, and supervisors. What I found was exactly what the company expected: that programmers did not see any need for the "writing tablet"; they were happy to continue coding programs on paper and sending their code down to the keypunch department, or hastily keypunching their own cards when they had to test programs in the middle of the night.

The writing tablet that I tried out was, according to the engineers I met, reliable up to 90 percent of the time.[7] It was ready to be tested and marketed. Why wasn't it introduced, and why did the programmers feel they didn't need it?

These questions are best answered with a continuation of the story. In the summer of 1993, Apple introduced a palm-sized portable device called the Newton. The Newton is, of course, a smaller and more sophisticated version of the early "writing tablet," one that not only recognizes handwriting but can send and receive wireless faxes and electronic mail, and also function as a pager. While the first Newton was notorious for its misrecognition of handwriting, the software has since been modified and now other manufacturers are jumping into the "palm-size" market with Personal Digital Assistants (PDAs) and "personal communicators."

Palm-size computers are finally catching on, although the emphasis is more on their role in mobile communications than on their writing-recognition capabilities. Like the writing tablet, they had to wait for changes in economic conditions, forms of work organization, and technological developments. An "invention" may be there, but it will not be adopted until the conditions for its use are established.

They didn't think it would sell![8]

• **In 1878** Alexander Graham Bell began to lay out plans for a national network of telephones. The president of Western Union and Telegraph turned down an offer to buy the patent rights to the telephone. "What use could this company make of an electronic toy?" he asked.

• **In the early 1950s,** Remington Rand built the UNIVAC computer. IBM rejected an offer to acquire the rights to this machine "because it felt that the greatest market potential for computers was in scientific rather than business applications."

• **In the late 1950s,** when the Xerox 914 copier was introduced, a major management-consulting firm predicted that the United States would need no more than 500 copiers at most.

BUREAUCRACY BLOSSOMS

The factory model of work and systems development also won out because it fit with management's view of how organizations should be run. Today, when television shows on money management and magazines like *Business Week* talk about the "virtual corporation" where independent workers show their "entrepreneurial spirit," it is easy to forget that there was similar hype in the 1970s about corporate rule-based behavior. This was a period when bureaucratic practices held sway as national and multinational businesses expanded, and magazines showered praise on U.S. corporations and their managerial practices. In fact, the financial success of these companies was said to be partly the result of the efficiency of their bureaucratic approach to management.

The bureaucratic approach divided workers into departments, managed by pastry-like layers of supervisors and managers. It also institutionalized office behavior, imposing impersonal rules for everything from proper office dress to forms of greeting. This was done through training, memos, meetings, and gearing salaries and promotions to annual or semi-annual reviews that rated employees on these criteria. Many of us who worked for large organizations learned to follow one set of practices to keep our jobs and set ourselves up for promotion, while talking and acting in other ways when it wasn't being "counted." Men, for example, would put their jackets on to go down the hall, while women would slip off their flat shoes and put on a pair of heels when going off to a meeting. In bureaucratic organizations, managers did not have to resort to hard-line threats like "Do it or you're fired" because workers were supposed to "know what was expected of them" and act accordingly. According to Richard Edwards, an economist, getting workers to follow bureaucratic procedures worked like this:

> The defining feature of bureaucratic control is the institutionalization of hierarchical power. "Rule of law"—the firm's law—replaces "rule by supervisor command."... Work becomes highly stratified; each job is given its distinct title and description; and impersonal rules govern promotion. "Stick with the corporation," the worker is told, "and you can ascend up the ladder."[9]

This form of control, which relied on employees taking responsibility for their own work within a well-specified rule structure, was particularly suited to the white-collar workforce, which was in general well educated and recruited from the ranks of white, middle-class Americans who had been brought up to believe in "getting ahead." Promotions, salary raises, and status symbols like offices with windows all depended on conforming to corporate rules, or at least knowing when they could be broken.

But dissatisfaction with the bureaucratic model was building. Workers at all levels of the office hierarchy began to demand some kind of job enrichment and more control over their working conditions. One executive cited in the 1973 *Work in America* report put it this way:

> You feel like a small cog. Working there was dehumanizing and the struggle to get to the top didn't seem worth it. They made no

effort to encourage your participation. The decisions were made in those rooms with closed doors.

The same reaction was apparent at the clerical level. This is how one college graduate expressed her dissatisfaction:

> I didn't go to school for four years to type. I'm bored, continuously humiliated. They sent me to Xerox school for three hours.... I realize that I sound cocky, but after you've been in the academic world ... and someone tries to teach you to push a button—you get pretty mad. They even gave me a goldplated plaque to show I've learned how to use the machine.[10]

Yet bureaucratic management is still very much alive. Magazines like *Business Week* may announce its death, but as anyone who works in an office knows, echoes of bureaucratic practices can be heard in today's carpeted cubicles. How did they become so well entrenched?

DIVIDED AND ALMOST CONQUERED

> The separation of hand and brain is the most decisive single step in the division of labor taken by the capitalist mode of production.
> —Harry Braverman, *Labor and Monopoly Capital*, 1974[11]

During the 1970s, division of labor within the labor process began to be debated by scholars and workers alike. The labor process is what economists refer to when they talk about how work is divided and who gets to do what. Although changes in the labor process may seem impersonal, the result of chance rather than design, they are in fact the result of the exercise of managerial control over the workplace, and particularly over its tasks and procedures.

In his pathbreaking 1974 book, *Labor and Monopoly Capital*, Harry Braverman offered an account of management's efforts to take control of the labor process. He argued that management needs to control the labor process not only in order to control costs but also in order to control workers.[12] By removing knowledge from workers—and therefore in essence taking away their skills—management creates a workforce that can be paid less, and one that is less likely to rebel and therefore easier to control. The changes in clerical and computer work, described in the last chapter, typified this process. These types of changes are the result of what Max Weber described as work *rationalization*, which meant breaking down each task into smaller and simpler steps, and creating specialized, narrow, and repetitive work procedures.

To management, the term rationalization has a positive value: by making work more "rational," it is also made more "sensible." But the use of such a positive-sounding term masks the fact that divided and specialized labor removes skills from the worker's control—something that is anything but sensible.

While many management consultants responded to the *Work in America* report by paying lip service to the need for more "humanistic" management,[13] Braverman argued that their strategies were essentially sugar-coating for rationalization, calling them a "style of management rather than a genuine change in the position of the worker." This was particularly true, he said, in offices where "office rationalization has in part been taking place, in the most recent period, under the banner of job enlargement and the humanization of work."[14] He went on to describe how consultants are called in to cut labor costs and "enhance" jobs: "In a typical case," he continued, "a bank teller who is idle when the load at the counter is light will be pressed into service handling other routine duties, such as sorting returned checks." The "Human Capital" school of management developed elaborate models of how training and enhanced skill would bring about a more productive workplace. But according to Braverman's analysis, work that had already been rationalized, as well as jobs that fit the back-office mold, was not effected by this rhetoric.

To better understand the division of labor that was applied to office work in the 1970s, Braverman takes us back to Charles Babbage and Frederick Taylor, two people who had strongly advocated detailed division of labor. Babbage, known as the father of the modern computer (see box, p. 46), made the case in the 1830s that there were great labor savings to be made from increasing specialization and a more and more detailed division of labor. Babbage's emphasis on saving labor costs set in motion the scientific management movement that grew in the early part of this century.

Frederick Taylor, the turn-of-the-century guru of scientific management, did time-and-motion studies of factory work in order to separate it into small tasks that management could organize. In his *Principles of Scientific Management*, published in 1911, Taylor put forth three principles. The first was that "The managers assume ... the burden of gathering together all of the traditional knowledge which in the past has been possessed by the workman and then classifying, tabulating, and reducing the knowledge to rules, laws, and formulae." In order to accomplish this remarkable feat of gathering knowledge from workers and bringing it under managerial control, Taylor laid out his second principle: "All possible brain work should be removed from the shop and centered in the planning or laying-out department." To make it all work, Taylor had a third principle, which Braverman describes as the "use of this monopoly over knowledge to control each step of the labor process and its mode of execution."[15]

The three principles are interconnected. The attempt to take skills away from workers by removing their control over the labor process is supplemented by the separation of conception (thought) from execution (action), which leaves workers with fewer defenses against managerial control strategies, including bureaucratic corporate practices. Taylor's techniques were thus a clear attempt to separate the head from the hands.

To modern ears, Taylor's principles of turning work into a series of cut-and-dried rationalized operations sound harsh and even unworkable. Yet the bulk of office tasks, particularly those in the back offices of banks, insurance companies, credit card processing facilities, and airlines, still follow procedures that take the form of Taylor's recommendations. There are countless examples of the application of these principles to office work. In the early 1970s, for example, Studs Terkel interviewed a telephone solicitor whose story provides a glimpse of how today's telephone-based occupations were to develop: "We didn't have to think what to say. They had it all written out. You have a card. You'd go down the list and call everyone on the card. You'd have about fifteen cards with person's names, addresses and phone numbers. 'This is Mrs. Du Bois. Could I have a moment of your time?'"[16]

In the language of work rationalization, the worker who does the same task over and over again, working from a prepared script as this telephone solicitor did, is being *deskilled* because she does not have a chance to use her own intelligence and knowledge. This is cheaper for the employer because, like piecework in the pre-assembly-line factory, the telephone solicitor is paid a low hourly wage plus a commission for each successful sale. In the telephone solicitor's case, the "dissociation" of the labor process from her skills diminished her sense of control over her work, leaving her feeling alienated. She continued: "The supervisor would sometimes listen in. He had connections with all the phones. ... If a new girl would come in, he'd have her listen to see how you were doing—to see how well this person was lying. That's what they taught you. After a while, when I got down to work, I wanted to cry."[17]

As early as the end of the eighteenth century, Adam Smith, the author of *The Wealth of Nations* and founder of modern economics, had warned that people become stifled in cut-and-dried jobs. In the nineteenth century Karl Marx argued that stifled workers would be, among other things, less productive. By the 1970s these projections were becoming as true for office work as they had been for factory production. The 1973 *Work in America* report noted that the cross-section of office employees surveyed were "producing at only 55 percent of their potential. Among the reasons cited for this was boredom with repetitive jobs."[18] Thus the separating of tasks done by the head (managers) from those done by the hands (workers) not only resulted in more boring work, but also cut down on potential productivity.

THE HEAD AND THE HANDS IN COMPUTER WORK

The 1970s was the decade in which management continued making office work more routine. Yet problems arose as workers were moved around like different parts in a machine. By the end of the decade many managers were finding that it was very difficult to successfully "deskill" office work because, among other things, they had finally recognized the fact that skill itself was hard to define.[19] Attempts at deskilling secretaries and receptionists often failed because managers and consultants never quite "got it": they did not understand the wide range of tacit and behind-the-scenes knowledge that these workers—who were, of course, mostly women—needed in order to accomplish even such "simple" tasks as composing a letter. Furthermore, while management practice separated clerical workers into pools and tried to routinize functions like data entry, there was no clear way to measure whether this form of work organization produced more or better documents.

This was equally the case with the design of word-processing machines and software for mainframe computers. Systems analysts tried to build on the assumption that data could be routinely processed, but the people doing the work often spent a lot of time trying to get around the stumbling blocks created by these routinized systems. In one office, for example, clerks complained about a problem that was prevalent during the period: they had trouble locating customers by computer-generated account numbers—in their daily work the clerks had been used to dealing with customers by name. Like the problems caused by assigning codes to welfare recipients, pre-assigned codes not only interfered with the way clerks worked, but they also interfered with efficient service as customers found themselves standing in line or waiting on the phone for longer periods of time.

Employees at an IRS service center, 1980s. They are entering data at "dumb" terminals that are hooked up to a mainframe. The use of dumb terminals to enter large volumes of data first became common in the 1970s. [UPI/Bettmann Newsphotos]

Yet what these systems, both managerial and technical, lacked in their ability to turn office work into factory-like procedures they made up for in terms of their success in putting the stamp of managerial control over the work process. If we go back to the example of programming work discussed in the last chapter, we can see how further divisions of labor were cemented into place during the 1970s. Now it was systems analysts who were increasingly split off from programmers. The analysts, as their title implied, were expected to take on more and more of the conceptual work, while the programmers were relegated to the more routine functions—tasks that were standardized, simplified, and cut up into modules or chunks of computer code to be written.

Once again, the split was between head and hands, between the higher paid work of systems analysis and the lower paid and (it was assumed) more routine work of writing program code. And once again major problems arose. The programmers were to write code based on written specifications the analysts had developed in discussions with customers. But the programmers complained that the specifications missed "real world" things, like filing customers by name instead of by number, or recognizing that many payroll transactions required special handling rather than routine, "automatic" processing. Because programmers weren't able to talk to customers directly, they often found that they were coding and recoding the same programs in an unproductive attempt to make them do what was needed.

But by splitting off analytical work, programming jobs were routinized and salaries were reined in. The average starting salary for programmers remained static from 1970 to 1972, instead of increasing as it had up to that point. In 1975, a survey found that the salaries of programmers in large institutions had increased only 2 percent over the previous year, failing to keep up with inflation.[20]

The routinization of programming, coupled with flatter salaries, gave management more control over the time, cost, and delivery of computer systems. This in turn set the stage for managers in the 1980s to order ready-made applications programs rather than hiring more programmers.

WINDS OF ECONOMIC CHANGE

In retrospect, we can see how routinized and divided tasks didn't necessarily turn out better documents or provide for faster service. Indeed, the way the work was divided, and the way computer systems were designed to reinforce this division, limited office workers' skills and their ability to get the job done. Similar problems arose in corporations that, by dividing and segmenting work, became weighed down with bureaucracy, causing slower movement in the choppy waters of international trade.

It is not just that management "styles" undergo change, but that any form of workplace activity, whether it comes from management or the workers, changes as external economic conditions (such as global competition) change and as internal contradictions bubble to the surface. During the 1970s, three large contradictions had surfaced: centralized bureaucratic operations were hindering business expansion; the extensive division of labor and the routinization of work were leading to worker dissatisfaction and evidence that productivity was not increasing; and software based on routine and repetitive coding functions was not applicable to smaller computers or to nonroutine transactions. Management theories in the 1970s had relied on two concepts that were considered central to economics—that economies of scale would bring economic success (bigger is better) and that intensive division of labor would result in faster and cheaper work activities. Both of these suppositions were to bend to the economic and political realities of the 1980s. And the move toward smaller organizations with less detailed division of labor called for different kinds of hardware and software.

4

THE 1980s: STUMBLING TOWARD "AUTOMATED" OFFICES

"They come in here every six months or so and reorganize us—
send us to seminars and focus groups on how important we are.
Then they put us back in our cubicles doing the same thing."
—Office worker, 1988

The terms "office automation," the "office of the future," and
the "paperless office" crept into the English language in the first
half of the 1980s. The office of the future was to be both automated and paperless, with computer disks acting as the new filing
system. The phrase office automation implied the continuous
and seamless processing of information, something like a factory
assembly line. Yet, except for back-office functions, which, as we
saw in the last chapter, had been rationalized in the 1960s and

1970s, there was very little that was "seamless" or smooth about the automation that went on in the 1980s. Indeed, it was a decade of contradictory predictions as well as practices. Some social scientists and managers believed that the spread of the personal computer would put an end to deskilling practices and herald the beginning of job enhancement and upgrading. Others argued that the incorporation of previously deskilled work into computer software meant continued deskilling, and also set the stage for reductions in employment. Both were partially right—depending on what part of the office you were looking at.

Offices in the 1980s looked quite different from their predecessors. For example, the 1988 film *Working Girl* showed an office overflowing with electronic equipment. In the opening shot Melanie Griffith, who plays a secretary to a group of securities traders, sits at a small desk that is crowded with a computer terminal (presumably to the stock market system) *and* a personal computer. In addition to looking differently, skills and rules changed in the 1980s. In the film, Griffith is a secretary who crosses the class line by "breaking the rules" and using knowledge of company trading in addition to her keyboarding skills. By the end of the movie, she has "made it" out of the open area of secretarial work stations into her own windowed office.

THE OFFICE OF THE FUTURE?

In terms of technology, the 1980s can best be seen as broken into two parts. The front office of the first half was not much different from the front office of the 1970s, with a few personal computers added to take care of clerical functions. It was not until the second half of the 1980s that personal computers spread up through the office hierarchy, accompanied by increasingly common fax machines, voice-mail systems, and other forms of office technology.

By mid-decade many stand-alone word-processing machines had been replaced by computers. But the early "office of the future" didn't look like the safe, clean, pleasant working environment that advertisements seemed to promise. The introduction of desktop computers was rather haphazard, reflecting the fact that managers weren't sure what they could be used for, or, in fact, where or how they should be used. In some offices, what seemed like miles of cable was run from machine to machine in a primitive attempt at networking. Many office workers complained about lack of space, and the situation only worsened as newer model PCs replaced outdated ones every eighteen months or so, leaving the older models sitting on file cabinets or stuffed awkwardly into bookcases. In addition to overcrowding, there was the serious problem of the decibel levels created by dot-matrix printers banging out printed pages. In many front offices these printers drowned out normal conversation, and the sound level in back offices was, as one word-processor put it, "thunderous." While ergonomic experts (specialists who study the fit between people and machines) recommended muffling the printer noise, little attention was paid to where the new PCs were placed, particularly when they were being used by clerical workers. And while carbon paper was a thing of the past, workers' hands were not necessarily any cleaner, because changing ribbons on the printers was a messy and time-consuming task. It wasn't until the later part of the decade that devices to buffer sound, like hoods and underpads, were widely introduced, along with ink cartridges instead of printer ribbons.

By the second half of the 1980s, computers had moved onto the desks of managers and professionals in most professions—with the exception of law firms and government offices, which were slow to jump on the PC bandwagon. Green and amber flickering screens (computer makers were still experimenting with which colors were easiest to see) were everywhere. At first, managers routinely complained that they had to rely on their secretaries to explain "how the thing worked." One middle-level manager voiced a concern that was repeated by many: "I didn't even know how to turn it on. And of course I didn't know how

Cubicles in an upscale office, early 1980s. Increasingly sophisticated in their use of space and storage facilities, such modules give management flexibility in restructuring the workplace. [Steelcase]

to type. All this 'Hit Shift, Command, Option' stuff had me confused. I'm really dependent on [my secretary] for getting out of tough situations."

The physical layout of the office also changed. It was at this point that the use of office cubicles really caught on. Cubicles had been around for several decades, but it was not until the 1980s that they were embraced by management strategists, perhaps because by then they fit in with plans for decentralized work. At the same time, sets of cubicles fit in with the notion of team work groups, as well as meeting the objective of squeezing more people into less space at a time when real estate costs were rising rapidly. They were successfully marketed by companies like Steelcase, Inc., a large supplier of office furniture, as a modular approach to office and organizational design. Modules complete with different-sized partition walls, upper and lower cabinet space, and a variety of fabric coverings provided not only sound barriers in crowded offices, but also indicated status by their size and color.

But while cubicles met cost objectives, they were not necessarily the best way to get work done. Many workers felt that they were being isolated and were losing the all-important sense of being able to talk to the person at the next desk. Such talking has a productive as well as social function, as it often is an important way of getting the job done. An insurance benefits analyst described her reorganized office this way:

> The office has become much more impersonal now, because we don't talk to each other. The girl who pays the Consolidated Underwriters' claim sits right in front of me. There was a question on my claim form. She didn't turn around and ask me. She sent me a letter. She didn't realize it was me.[1]

By the end of the decade, cubicle walls, like personal computers, were a common feature of the office. But they were only the external features marking other changes in the design, development, and marketing of software that made this possible.

ENTER THE (NOT VERY) PERSONAL COMPUTER

Microcomputers, or what later came to be called personal computers or desktop computers, had been around since the 1970s, when electronics buffs bought kits in order to build their own machines. By the early 1980s, Atari, an early manufacturer of microcomputers, had produced an array of educational software, as well as the games it has since become famous for. Apple also came on the scene at this time, marketing to homes and schools.

In the office market, Wang and Xerox sold word-processing machines that included specialized hardware and built-in software. During the early part of the decade "knowing the Wang or the Xerox" was considered a strong job-hunting skill for a secretary or office assistant. In addition, there were a number of companies that manufactured general-purpose microcomputers (as opposed to specialized machines, like Wang's word-processors), although there were few software programs available for them and software companies had not yet begun mass marketing directly to businesses.

In 1982, IBM jumped into the microcomputer market by introducing its "personal computer." These were much like other computers at the time: the difference was in IBM's sales force and marketing strategy, which aimed at offices rather than homes and schools. As it had with its keypunch equipment and mainframe computers in the 1960s and 1970s, IBM used its already established corporate connections to win a foothold in the office market—telling managers that the best thing was to stay with the company they knew.

Only this time several things went wrong: IBM not only misjudged what its computers would and could be used for, but in emphasizing hardware it left software, training, and work reorganization by the wayside. It was also vulnerable to being pushed out of the hardware market by lower priced compatible computers, or "clones." Perhaps the only aspect of IBM's first move into personal computers that seemed to stick was the name "PC." This is, in retrospect, a strange name since they were targeted at the office market.

The PC carried over the antiquated QWERTY keyboard design from the typewriter. In the last century, the QWERTY keyboard—named for the letters on the left side of the top row—was designed to slow typists down so that the keys wouldn't stick together when they sprang up from the typewriter and struck the paper. By the early 1980s, there were over 3 million clerical workers with keyboard experience. Rather than rock the boat by introducing both computers and a redesigned keyboard, designers stuck with the typewriter format.

Although much of the history of technology focuses on hardware, it was the development of software applications in the 1980s that sparked personal computer use. The story of Visicalc, the first spreadsheet program, is widely known to early computer users. The spreadsheet was a fairly simple program that arranged numbers in rows and columns, adding up the totals and calculating percentages and averages. It was generally credited with having been the program that made professionals see the value of using computers. In particular, many accountants, auditors, and supervisors were quick to find out that they could use it to set up budgets, track sales, and keep records and statistics. Spreadsheet programs like Excel and Lotus have followed the Visicalc model, and today remain near the top of the list of best-selling programs.

Word-processing software, also widely used in the early 1980s, was not so quickly adopted into managerial and professional occupations. Part of the problem was that word-processing programs were designed for secretaries, and the designers seem to have *assumed* that secretaries merely input what their bosses had written. Early word-processing programs were therefore designed for input speed rather than for formatting and editing. This was also the result of the failure of technical specialists to take seriously the "invisible skills"—like rewording and editing—that were being used in what was considered women's work. WordStar, for example, the first big-selling word-processing program for the PC, had hopelessly complex sets of commands (using the Shift, Control, and Function keys in different combinations), combined with the next-to-impossible-to-remember letters that were used with the function keys (like "∧G" for erasing a character). But its major flaw was that it separated supposedly routine functions like entering text from more editorial ones like formatting and rearranging—the classic separation of head from hands.

An accountant using an early personal computer, 1985. Spreadsheets, one of the first computer applications, performed calculations rapidly, helping to popularize the use of PCs in the office. [Jim West]

COORDINATE AND CONTROL

Management's function is to coordinate and control divided labor, pulling together various departments of head and hand work. By the end of the 1970s, it had become clear to management that the extensive division of labor used in most large organizations was leading to worker dissatisfaction, no gains in productivity, and decreased control over quality. According to the business press, the United States, the leader in post-industrial development, was now looking over its shoulder at what was being called the "Japanese challenge." Many management experts began to recommend that instead of further centralization, companies should begin to *decentralize*—spreading out coordination and operations functions. It was also suggested that there would be fewer coordination problems if there was *less* division of labor and more collapsing of job titles.[2] It was not that management objectives had changed: the basics of reducing labor costs and increasing productivity were still paramount. But the underlying assumption behind large, centralized workplaces—that they should be organized around "economies of scale"—was being challenged by decentralized, scaled-down production strategies. The realization that Japan might be succeeding with smaller scale manufacturing, particularly in auto production, turned management's eyes in that direction.

Not everyone agreed that keeping up with the Japanese was the correct solution. For one thing, it was an open question whether Japan's decentralized "lean" factory production strategies were appropriate for U.S. offices. For another, it was not clear that there was a known strategy for fitting job design and technology together. In a study commissioned by the U.S. Congress, the Office of Technology Assessment found that simply moving organizational pieces around did not work:

> Where organizational issues like job redesign and workflow re-structuring have not been properly managed, organizational costs can more than offset productivity gains expected from new technology. A number of firms were demonstrably *worse off with automation* than they were without it, at least in the short run.[3]

In other words, organizational restructuring and office automation had to be planned and made to fit together. And there was no existing model, Japanese or otherwise, that showed how this should be done.

Throughout the 1980s, the traditional reliance on centralized, rationalized policies existed side-by-side with the newer decentralized operations; back-office operations generally followed the 1970s practice of centralization and rationalization, while front-office functions, particularly professional and analytical jobs, were more likely to be decentralized. Yet both remained built on the historical base of bureaucratic rule-based practices.

Management theorists argued that in order to make decisions swiftly in an expanding global market, the threads of bureaucratic control had to unravel, along with the fabric of hierarchical chain-of-command rules. Management experts today like to say that U.S. companies should have gotten rid of bureaucratic overhead and "downsized" sooner. But even in restructured organizations, the essence of bureaucracy—its reliance on self-disciplined workers who have internalized corporate rules—remains intact, as have the control systems upper management developed in the heyday of corporate and governmental bureaucracy.

NETWORKS AND "USERS"

> In 1980 virtually all of corporate computing power was in main-frames, and in 1987, 95 percent of corporate computing power was in desktop PCs.
>
> —*Forbes*, 1993[4]

The shift from mainframes to PCs brought with it technical changes that reflected managerial policy about workplace reorganization. An intermediate step between the mainframe and the PC was the minicomputer, which also came into widespread use in the 1980s. Minicomputers, which cost less than mainframes, also took up less space, were easier to operate, and were used to set up networks. They became the workhorses in the move to decentralize corporate departments and their computer services. This change gave departmental managers and computer center directors more say about the work that could be carried out within their realms; it also gave more workers access to computers and potentially gave them greater access to information as well.

Minicomputers are still around, but they were soon matched in speed and storage capacity by PCs. By the end of the 1980s, minicomputers were being replaced by high capacity PCs that acted as file servers (work stations that function as switching stations) into Local Area Networks, or LANs, have decentralized PC use still further. As one technical analyst put it, "People don't have to beg for information any more." LANs fit the bill by fitting into flatter organizations that could support decentralized decision-making.

But while LANs in theory solved the problem of how to spread information through large decentralized organizations, in practice managers and technical specialists had to deal with a technological Tower of Babel: too many pieces of hardware couldn't be used together, while "protocols" (hardware and software interfaces) lagged far behind. Software, particularly the operating systems that direct the flow of information between and among computers and input/output devices, lacked industry-wide standards, making it very difficult to share files and information. For much of the decade, management philosophy, workplace practices, and technical achievement were out of sync.

Many office workers who began using computers in this period remember the frustration of trying to get a disk from one computer to work on another, or simply trying to get something printed out from someone else's printer. Rush jobs, a common office phenomenon, often ran into the evening as files were lost in temporarily wired-together networks, or disappeared due to "disk error." This was time-consuming as well as frustrating, with clerical workers, professionals, and managers often saying that doing something on the computer took more time than it would have by hand.

Systems analysts and directors of Management Information Systems (MIS) departments tried to get around these hardware and software problems by designing new systems from scratch. But here too there were missteps and missed cues because they often focused on the wrong problem. For the developers of computer systems, the decade was one of discovering the "user," the name given by computer specialists to those who used the machines.[5] A focus on user issues began to dominate computer management and system development literature, but most books, articles, and seminars addressed the issue of how to "integrate the user" into the system, not how the system could serve the user. In the 1970s, development literature focused too heavily on routinized systems and rationalized procedures, failing to acknowledge people. Now, while beginning to actually look at people, they were still ignoring how those people worked.[6]

The goal of designing "idiot proof" systems (computer programs that made it almost impossible to hit the wrong function key) was another theme of managers and system developers in this period. Particularly in the area of custom-designed applications for back-office operations, systems analysts were warned to keep the number of steps down to a minimum so that any "idiot" could learn to use the program—missing the point that much back-office work involved the invisible work of making decisions and setting priorities.

Furthermore, most software was tested in controlled laboratories rather than actual workplaces. This meant that designers missed the complexity of real-life work, where several tasks are taken on at once.[7] Lab testing can't catch common issues, such as the fact that we may be answering the phone at the same time we are responding to a "prompt" from a software application. If, for example, the "prompt" asks if we should save a file, and we hit the Enter key instead of typing "Yes," the result can be many hours of lost work.

In the later half of the decade, a rising chorus of critics among both computer professionals and user groups argued that software had to be tested in actual workplace environments in order to find out, in advance, what was likely to go wrong with the "fit" between how the software was designed and how it was used. Similarly, the emphasis on "idiot-proof" systems began to fade as such systems, particularly those used by insurance companies and banks, often resulted in clerical workers having to waste time by flipping through multiple screens.

THE ART OF SYSTEM DEVELOPMENT

In hindsight, the idea that idiot-proof and lab-tested systems could actually be effective seems shortsighted, yet this notion dominated system development in the 1980s and still hovers in the background today. Indeed, hardware and software problems of the sort just described were more a failure to recognize actual work practices than they were technical failures. To better understand how this happened, it is useful to know a little more about the theory and practice of system development.

Systems development literature, including widely known books by such authors as Edward Yourdon, Tom DeMarco, and Michael Jackson, calls on system designers to mimic the physical sciences by being "objective" and "isolating the problem."

Yourdon, who like DeMarco and Jackson has a large management consulting practice, defines his design strategy as one "that breaks large complex problems into smaller less complex problems and then decomposes each of these smaller problems into even smaller problems, until the original problem has been expressed as some combination of many small solvable problems."[8]

These routine procedures are not in the least aimed at designing systems that real people can use in real situations. The consultants' approach looks at *information flow* rather than social relationships, *problems* instead of workplace situations, personnel-file *skill descriptions* rather than tacit knowledge, and *rule-based procedures* over on-the-job experience.[9] Essentially, real work is made invisible by these procedures.

What these approaches lack in originality and human orientation they make up for in cost-control procedures and control over the management of information. As in the 1970s, the main complaint of the managers who were buying programming services was that custom-designed software was too expensive and took too long to be delivered. The structured systems approach— the name given to the methods used by Yourdon and others— promised to deliver more predictable software on time and within budget. The "bottom line" therefore took priority over finding ways to develop computer systems that would better fit the work.

Take the case of data-entry clerks who enter health insurance claim information. The supposedly "idiot-proof" processing systems they use have been designed to accept or reject claims on the basis of the codes they enter. Although a fair amount of judgment goes into entering and assigning codes, with clerks often having to refer to medical reference lists or call doctors' offices, many insurance computer systems have been designed with the assumption that entering codes is a routine function, and one that can be speeded up by designing data-entry screens that call for only codes, with no further explanations. By ignoring work practices and instead focusing on units of data (like medical codes), system analysts not only get the systems designed faster but they also speed up the work of the claims processors. The result is a system that rejects more claims than it accepts—the bottom of the bottom line, because the insurance company can pay out less to customers.

AUTOMATING AND "INFORMATING" OFFICES

In *The Age of the Smart Machine*, Shoshana Zuboff, a well-known social scientist, argued that centralized, rationalized policies would lead to computer systems that would be "automating" the workplace, while decentralized, enhancement schemes could lead to systems that would be "informating" work. Zuboff and others are strong advocates of the informating strategy, which they believe can, when combined with managerial decisions on job design, result in better and more meaningful jobs:

> While it is true that computer-based automation continues to displace the human body and its know-how (a process that has come to be known as *deskilling*), the informating power of the technology simultaneously creates pressure for a profound *reskilling*.[10]

Informating, in Zuboff's view, would mean using information technology to enhance and upskill, giving responsibility and knowledge back to those doing the work—in other words, using new forms of work organization and newer office technologies to set back the clock on rationalization and deskilling.

But while this faith in upskilling did filter up to front-office and professional jobs, most work that had already been divided remained automated and either relegated to isolated parts of buildings or hidden behind cubicle partitions. Why was this so? If social science, management policy, and computer technology *could* have been used to bring about more integrated, reskilled jobs, why was this more talked about than implemented?

The answer to these questions lies in the contradiction between informating practices that would humanize work and management policies that are aimed at lowering labor costs. In the 1980s, the movement to lower labor costs took on new momentum and, as a result, work was further divided or recombined so that it could be done with fewer workers. The newer policies were coated in the rich language of "enhancing human resources," making it seem that much was being done to improve skills and jobs. But as employment figures and salaries in the 1990s illustrate, management continued the rationalization of tasks and jobs that had already been standardized and simplified, while at the same time identifying new tasks and functions (like paraprofessional and analytical jobs) that could be molded into standardized forms. By the end of the 1980s, it was possible to use more reliable software to reintegrate previously rationalized tasks and standardized services. And the way to put work organization together with software was to create standard products and services. In this round of cost-cutting, the emphasis was not only on making workers and software more predictable, but on carving up services so that they too would be standardized and predictable.

REDEFINING PRODUCTS AND SERVICES

There is an adage in economics that says that "It is not possible to greatly increase the number of haircuts a barber can give in an hour." In other words, it is very difficult to raise productivity in the service sector. On the surface, this might seem to be true, but if the definition of either service or product is changed, then it might be possible to increase production. For instance, McDonald's changed the meaning of meal production by mass-producing the new "service" of fast food, thus making it possible to "produce" more hamburgers in an hour. In fact, hairdressers standardized and simplified hair styles in the early 1970s when they introduced the "cut-and-blow-dried" look —which meant that they were able to "produce" more haircuts per hour.

In the 1980s, this strategy of redefining services became established in banks, insurance companies, airlines, hotels, and government agencies. Like Henry Ford's Model T and Wonder Bread's sliced loaf, products in the service sector could be predetermined and measured, so that they could be produced faster and for less. In the office sector, this was particularly true for back-office functions.

Automated telephone response systems, introduced in the later part of the 1980s, are a classic example of a standardized and rationalized service. When a customer calls the office, he or she is given a range of pre-selected "options." Each option—which is chosen by pushing a number button—puts you through a defined channel to a person doing a specialized function. The customer service representatives who do these jobs are often located in an office far from headquarters. Their jobs have already been routinized and standardized to follow scripts. In *The Electronic Sweatshop*, Barbara Garson quotes an airline reservation agent who has been given a script to sell airline tickets:

> There's AHU, that's After Hang Up time. It's supposed to be fourteen seconds. It just came down to thirteen. But my average is five seconds AHU, because I do most of the work while the customer's still on the phone. There's your talk time, your availability, your occupancy—that's the percent of time you're plugged in, which is supposed to be 98 percent ...[11]

But, as with industrial production, not all products and jobs can be rationalized. In banking, for example, many new services, such as variable-rate mortgages, require customized, in-person attention from customer service representatives. Mortgage information can be built into a database, but it is up to the bank representatives to explain and "sell" it to the customer. And in the airline industry, travel agents provide a fuller range of non-standard services than the airlines do. But, as we will see in the next chapter, some of these new services came under the knife of rationalization in the 1990s, this time under the banner of reengineering.

Speeding up the pace of work was an intended consequence of standardizing services and software. Up until this period, profes-

Phone company operators handling repair calls, 1990. Across the country, such operators are rapidly being replaced by automated telephone response systems. [Jim West]

sional work had not been timed or monitored because it was assumed to require thinking, and commonsense held that thinking could not be measured. But this too was to change in the 1980s. "Everyone expects everything yesterday" became as common a complaint among professional and managerial staff as it had been among clerical workers. In part this was due to the proliferation of fax machines, voice mail, and software applications like data bases and spreadsheets that are expected to produce results "right away." But it was also the result of changing the definition of professional work to bring it more in line with measured results and standardized services. An analyst with a municipal agency put it this way:

At first they wanted more reports from me. You know, "plug in" the statistics and crank out the graphs. Then it turned out that longer reports were expected. And of course the reports have to be typed perfectly and be beautiful.

The analyst, like many professional workers, found that in order to get the work done, he had to work longer and harder—an intensification of work that was to take on monumental proportions in the 1990s.[12] He was also experiencing the clericalization of professional work which continues today, as more professionals and managers are expected to do their own word-processing and handle their phones and email.

In clerical jobs, what seemed at first to be little changes produced tremendous increases in the pace of work. These "small changes" included no longer having to get up to put a piece of paper in the typewriter, file a document, mail a letter, or look up information in a manual. In addition, having keystrokes counted sped up the pace for many back-office clerical workers. By the second half of the decade, carpel tunnel syndrome, which is the result of repetitive motion at the keyboard, as well as eye strain and severe headaches from staring at a computer screen all day, were illnesses that were beginning to be acknowledged.

Another consequence of standardization was managements' ability to move work around to wherever wages were less. Indeed, a branch of software design called Computer Support for Cooperative Work (CSCW) developed in this period, with one of its objectives being the development of programs that could be used to "support" workers sitting in different places. This mobility of work had been a key characteristic of Japanese "lean" production and was put into place by the U.S. auto industry in its push toward the "global factory." In the office sector it was typified by the proliferation of 800 numbers for everything from bank balances to software technical support and professional services like taxes. Translating complex, in-person services into the more routine procedural steps of telephone "scripts" meant that this kind of work could be moved anywhere and done at any time. It also meant that corporate headquarters, which had moved from the central cities to the suburbs in the 1970s, were able to move further away from the reach of inner-city and minority workers in the 1980s.[13] And all of these issues were deeply intertwined with continuing discussions about skill.

TO SKILL OR BE DESKILLED, IS THAT THE QUESTION?

In the 1970s, Braverman's critical analysis of rationalized work processes led to scholarly and workplace discussions about the negative effects of deskilling. In the 1980s, these dialogues continued in the form of "skills debates," where some argued that newer forms of work organization and technology could bring about the rise of the "knowledge worker"—the person who could use all sorts of information technology.[14] Knowledge work was the epitome of upgraded and integrated work, with skill expectations higher and job content more challenging. But the dark side of knowledge work could be seen in the still increasing number of support staff jobs, where although people were using more information technology and taking on more responsibility, this was not reflected in rising wages or in higher status or promotional opportunities.

Just as centralized and decentralized corporate structures existed side by side, so too did jobs that were being deskilled or rationalized coexist with upskilled or "knowledge worker" jobs. To better understand this process of polarized skill, it is useful to take a look at the broader aspects of skill, beginning with an understanding of how managers plan job design and work organization.

Tasks and responsibilities are two aspects of what economists call *job content*, and they change as work is reorganized. In this period, managers and consultants advocated broadening job content, which brought with it increasing skill requirements. An example of this can be found in *Brave New Workplace*, where Robert Howard tells the story of a "what if" scenario in a large bank. Before work reorganization, one letter-of-credit department worker said of his job, "You used to do one job continuously. You could go a little crazy it was so boring."[15] Management hired a consultant who suggested that rather than using computers as if this was a factory assembly line, work could be organized differently. Howard describes the consultant's concept this way:

> What if, instead of dividing up the tasks in the back office, they were woven together into a coherent whole? What if, in the letter-of-credit office, for example, each worker handled the *entire* issuing process from start to finish for one customer or specific set of customers, rather than repeating the same isolated task for them all? And what if technology was used to support this redesign of work, rather than simply freezing the inefficient organization already in place?[16]

Some would see the suggested reorganization as the new humanistic management style, integrating tasks and proposing job enhancement or "upskilling." Indeed, it was made in the early 1980s, a time when government deregulation was pushing banks to explore new markets. This in turn called for some new products and services, new computer systems, and a reorganized labor process, which some saw as job enhancement. But the changes also contained another characteristic, one that was to become all too common:

> By simplifying and "cleaning up" the work process, the department would *require fewer workers and labor costs would plummet.* By giving those workers *who remained* more responsibility in meeting the needs of customers, more training in the new technology, and higher salaries, both worker motivation and quality of work would improve. And by putting together the pieces of the back-office puzzle, jobs would become more skilled, more challenging, and more satisfying than ever before.[17]

Yes, more challenge and responsibility for some clerical workers, but fewer workers overall, meeting the objective of cutting total labor costs.

The results of these strategies were unfortunately all too predictable. Since women and minorities did a high percentage of the work that was "automated out," they bore the brunt of this change. In 1982, for example, over 80 percent of the more than 18 million clerical workers were women. Of these, the three job categories with more than 20 percent minority workforces—keypunch operators, mailroom clerks, and file clerks—were not only the lowest paid but were among the first to be cut.[18]

Skill is closely linked to job content. In the late 1980s, skills were integrated into computer systems at all levels within organizations, but with noticeably different effects. Shoshana Zuboff, linking skill with her idea of "informating" work, explains how computer systems *could* be used to increase skill levels in clerical positions:

> Activities that had once been extracted from the professional domain and rationalized in lower level jobs could now be reintegrated with those higher level positions. For example, bank workers could interact directly with the data base, perform analyses, and develop ideas. The remaining clerical positions would take on a quasi-professional status, requiring information management and business knowledge.[19]

The scenario Zuboff sketches has come to be called the "professionalization of clerical work," the flip side of professionals getting to do "clericalized" work. A problem with it, however, is that it is implemented only when managers (or the army of consultants they hire) are able to show that *overall* labor costs are decreasing and that the remaining people are producing more. Another problem with this more rosy skill-enhancement scenario is the fact that the invisible dimension of a clerical worker's skill—the harder to quantify, more tacit aspects of the job—rarely gets included in job descriptions or evaluations.[20] Thus when it comes time to make clerical work more professional, workers may be expected to perform with more skills, but won't necessarily be compensated for the new knowledge and skill they bring to the job. As we will see, this is particularly true of computer skills.

The 1980s were a time when there were a number of organizational and technical alternatives to rationalized, bureaucratic work practices. Yet these possible choices faded as management reined in labor costs and used office technology to further control both costs and work processes. In 1985, Congress's Office of Technology Assessment conducted a series of case studies of different industries in order to study changes in office technology, employment patterns, job training, organizational structures, job content, and skill. They argued that it wasn't the technology that was shaping changes in skill and job content, but rather the choices that were being made. The report, called *Automation of America's Offices*, stressed that by mid-decade changes in work were bringing about shifting power relations between management and the workforce. "These shifts in power depend less on the characteristics of the technology than on the characteristics of the organization and its management strategy."[21] Their predictions, grounded in careful analysis, pointed to changes that have since occurred. In general, they believed that the workplace developments of the early part of the 1980s would become more pronounced in the following decade. Specifically, they pointed to the increasing readiness of management to reduce labor costs by reducing back-office jobs; to limit the growth of middle-management jobs; and to spread work to part-time and temporary workers, as well as to move it out of the city and out of the country. In the 1990s, top management strategists were able to begin reengineering the workplace in order to carry out these changes more smoothly. We now turn to an examination of how the principles of reengineering combined organizational and technical change in order to bring about changes in jobs and reduced employment.

5

THE 1990s:
REENGINEERING
THE OFFICE

"It's not that you're being fired; it's the job that's being elimi-
nated."

—District manager, AT&T, 1994[1]

In 1990 and 1991 a recession masked structural job shifts—
shifts that were bringing about huge cuts in the number of
"payroll" or full-time jobs, a compression of job titles in those
that remained, and a surge in the "contingent" or "off-the-pay-
roll" workforce. These three changes were coupled with the
increasingly common phenomenon of people working from
home, both as "telecommuters" (on the payroll) and as
freelancers. All of these changes were propelled in part by the
practice of reengineering (see box on "Office Speak," p. 24),

which was used to flatten organizational hierarchies, reorganize work processes, redefine required skills, and introduce new technologies. The corporate way of organizing work, with its job ladders and relatively secure jobs, was being replaced by a return to the "entrepreneurial" ideal—where workers would fend for themselves. And last but not least, the restructured world of work was held in place through computer and communications networks, as well as by other now familiar varieties of office technology.

In the 1950s, C. Wright Mills wrote about political spokesmen who "exploit anxieties under the banner of free competition." By the 1990s, the effects of the division of labor, work reorganization, and recession, coupled with the impact of technology, meant that workers were now being pushed to further absorb these anxieties. Joshua Freeman, a labor historian, noted that restructuring left "no structure to deal with the new anxiety and uncertainty."[2] Meanwhile President Clinton's Secretary of Labor, Robert Reich, sounded an alarm by referring to what he called the "anxious class," which he explained was made up of "millions of Americans who no longer can count on having their jobs next year, or next month, and whose wages have stagnated or lost ground to inflation."[3]

FLEXIBLE WORKERS

Jobs don't change overnight. Patterns of reorganization build on prior structural changes. Here are examples of changes in the 1990s from the two occupational areas discussed in Chapters 2 and 3—computer jobs and clerical work—that still employ people in more or less traditional office settings. First we take a look at the new twists in programming work, which have reintegrated some programming, analysis, and management functions, but with the result that, like the trends we saw beginning slowly in the 1980s, these jobs were now being done by fewer people working longer hours and doing more tasks.

In 1994, when I interviewed Jack, a project manager in the information services division of a large industrial company, he had to drag a co-worker's chair into the hallway outside his cubicle so I could have a place to sit. "There are rules about office size," he explained, "but since we moved here three years ago, the whole technical staff has been pissed off because we have too much equipment and no place to put it. There isn't even enough space for our power cords."

The crowded conditions directly affect productivity in the office. "How is a programmer supposed to write code, for example, when he is sitting on the other side of a thin wall from a sales person who is on the phone all day?"

The information services division, which sells software for electronic interchange systems and has about 2,500 employees worldwide, is a profit center for this industrial giant. In the last few years it has been undergoing a major reorganization. "We used to have twenty levels of titles, but in 1986-1987 they jumbled them up and squeezed us into three 'career bands.'" Like similar "broad-banding" efforts in other large organizations, Jack's division now has administrative/support, technical/professional, and managerial "bands." As a project manager, he is part of the technical/professional band; management positions start higher up in the organizational chart. Middle managers have been cut, as have secretaries and most support staff. Jack doesn't think that the bands have affected salaries much, but since it is company policy not to discuss this, he isn't really sure. It is clear that raises are effectively smaller, however, because "they have lengthened the time between salary reviews from 12 to 14 or 16 months."

For Jack, a senior technical person with nine years in the company, the real change began about two years ago when they began assigning each project manager more than one project at the same time. "It's not like they want us to complete a project faster," he explains, "but it's an increase in the pace of work because we are working on so many things at once."

I've talked with Jack several times since that interview. He has often had to work late, "pulling bugs" out of programs—programs that he has written and programs that he is responsible for. As a project manager, he does just about everything, from coding programs to going around with salespeople and talking to customers. Perhaps he is the 1990s equivalent of the "jack of all trades," but without a better salary or control over his working environment.

The work that Jack and other project managers do is less divided than management had, in earlier periods, believed that it should be. In fact, despite prior waves of rationalization, project management has always involved a little analysis and programming—even in the 1970s, when top-level managers firmly believed that they had divided the work. But the changes of the 1990s have led to project leaders being responsible for all these tasks without a clear line of authority or pay for doing them. More can be done with fewer people because the work is based on structured programming languages and standardized system development tools that were developed in the 1980s. From top management's perspective, what couldn't be done by dividing and standardizing the work can now be accomplished by using more standardized tools and techniques.

Clerical work has also changed, and at least two patterns are emerging. The first, described through the story of Darleen, a former secretary/office manager, illustrates an opening that has allowed clerical workers to use and develop more skills. Darleen worked her way up to "producer" in a small store-front insurance agency. According to Darleen, a producer (a title we generally lump together with that of insurance agent) does everything from bookkeeping to selling and writing insurance policies. Like Jack's work, it is in an "all-round" occupation.

It's 8:30 in the morning and the phones are not turned on until 9:00, which gives Darleen time to catch up on her paperwork.

The back-office of a large corporation, 1990s. The dumb terminals of the 1970s and 1980s have been replaced by PCs, which have then been linked into Local Area Networks (LANs). [Steelcase]

Last night, after the phones were switched to the answering machine, she spent an hour and a half clearing up her desk.

"Normally my desk is one big pink slip," she says, nodding at the now neatly piled stacks of pink telephone messages. The computer monitor blinks by her right elbow. "The carrier [the insurance company] has a plan to switch us to paperless within two years."

Darleen went through an intensive insurance course in order to become licensed to sell insurance, but her training must continue. In addition to having to obtain 48 insurance company credits every four years in order to renew her license, she is expected to keep up with the legal changes, as well as the computer "system enhancements," that the carrier sends in. "I get home, get the kids fed, bathed, and hopefully in bed, and then after they ask for the sixth or seventh cup of water, I pick up the books, and FYI's [printouts from the carriers' email system]," she says. Darleen's co-worker jokes that she keeps a pad and pencil in the bathroom to jot down ideas she gets when she's in the shower, but Darleen says that's no joke. "I'm so tired at night," she explains, "that I have to pace around the living room while I read the printouts or else I fall asleep on the couch."

Darleen's job is an example of the "professionalization of clerical work." She earns more money and uses a wider range of knowledge and skills than she used to. But the working conditions and stress make it hard for her to spend time with her children and almost impossible to relax at work. Like a professional, she is expected to sharpen her skills on her own time, but with a take-home salary of $28,000, she doesn't experience the prestige or income that generally comes from professional work. Darleen is a single parent, with two small children, and her childcare expenses come to $13,000 a year—almost half her take-home income. The agency now functions without an office manager or secretary, and like the insurance company that it is connected to, operational cost savings are expected to come from eliminating clerical jobs and from people working harder.

The second clerical pattern can be seen in the work of Sandy, a customer service representative. This pattern is typical of what is happening in back offices, where tasks are being integrated into jobs that require more skill but whose wages do not reflect this.

Sandy sits in a reasonably sized, low-walled cubicle and is surrounded by about 350 other customer service representatives. When she stands up from her ergonomically designed chair, she has a clear view of trees and sky out through the large windows that surround the suburban building's open floor plan. She works for an 800-line operation in a large bank.

From the moment she sits down and keys her ID number into the automated call distributor (phone system), she is on-line and monitored. As calls come in, she pulls up customer records on her multi-windowed screen and goes to work sorting out customer problems. Queries can range from a request for an account balance (although most of these are handled by the totally automated voice-response system) to complicated problems where Sandy needs to test her "listening skills" so that she can help the caller identify his or her concerns and unravel whatever has gone awry with the account. In addition to handling customer service calls, representatives are encouraged to "sell" new bank products, such as certificates of deposit, to the customers who call.

Training for the job was intensive, with almost a month of full-time in-house courses and several weeks at a "training hall," where "team trainers" listened in and talked her through each call. Now team trainers, supervisors, and quality control experts—three levels of monitors—listen in to a certain percentage of her calls and give her a monthly rating on how well she is doing. She is evaluated on the number of calls handled per hour, and on a variety of quality characteristics that zero in on her level of courtesy, clarity, and accuracy in giving out information. Good ratings bring silver stars—actually, balloons that float over the cubicles—and a certain number of silver stars mean a cash prize. Starting pay is around $19,000 a year.

Sandy calls her work "boring" and "numbing," but acknowledges that it calls for a whole lot of skills, from listening to and counseling customers to a great deal of problem solving. She, like her co-workers, takes the computer system for granted, navigating her way through a warren of screens and windows, trying to out-guess customers as to which screen they may need next. While she is not at all pleased with the pay, the benefits (including health and a tuition refund plan) are a big attraction.

Sandy's manager knows that the job is a high-stress one and that the skill requirements are high. The 800-number service is being used to reroute customers who would otherwise call or go to their local branches, so that the number of service reps is expanding while the number of tellers and branch platform personnel is going down. The manager notes that despite the low salary, announcements of job openings draw a large pool of applicants, including lawyers and former middle managers who have been "downsized" out of their firms. "They want the benefits," she explains.

Telephone-based customer service work appears to be a growing job category.[4] Essentially, it integrates back-office functions with front-office customer relations functions—without the in-person contact. Much of this work, like Sandy's, is subject to close monitoring, which has been built into telephone and computer systems. Productivity meets management expectations as workers answer twenty-two calls an hour according to set criteria included in the monitoring. Calls are monitored, for example, on how well representatives stated the scripted opening and closing remarks, and how completely they informed the customer about each transaction. This couldn't have been accomplished if each part of a phone call and each aspect of bank work hadn't first been rationalized and defined. It also couldn't have been done unless customers were used to this kind of standardized "service."

The work that Jack, Darleen, and Sandy do is rooted in their having a firm footing in using and being comfortable with computer applications. But it also requires some complex juggling, so that a wide variety of skills and knowledge are compressed into every working hour. Some would say that this represents a break with the rationalization and deskilling patterns of the 1960s and 1970s. Yet in today's context, it is part of the continuing process of redesigning jobs.

REENGINEERED JOBS AND LIVES

Reengineering involves a form of work rationalization never imagined by Frederick Taylor and the old scientific management experts. In Taylor's day, there were few machines that could be counted on, and those that were useful were more like individual tools than mechanized systems. Thus Taylor's scientific management studies had to separate and freeze each step of a job so that it could be done faster by a person—early scientific management proponents could not rely on mechanization to do this. Now, after a long history of automating both factory and office work, managers have a greater range of strategies to call upon. Reengineering and its components are part of a toolbox of techniques that give top management more control over which jobs can be standardized, which can be combined, and which can be integrated through office technology.

Phrases like "leaner and meaner," "team players," "no pain, no gain," and "work smarter, not harder" make the downsizing process sound as if a team sport. Linking sports metaphors with the often dehumanizing process of reengineering not only heightens the competitive atmosphere, but makes it sound like the process is supposed to be fun—once again hiding the difficulties in an optimistic-sounding set of words.

In theory, reengineering calls for organizing the labor process so that costs can be saved by cutting out steps and organizational units. Darleen's and Sandy's work, with its emphasis on reintegrating tasks back into computer systems, is part of this process. Jack's work incorporates other reengineering principles, particularly in the way the organization has been regrouped into three "bands" of workers, instead of a large number of titles and job grades.

Management experts claim that reengineering is not the same as downsizing or eliminating jobs. Many argue that reengineering should make the organization more competitive and thus create new jobs in other areas. But this, like the technological leap of faith discussed earlier, requires suspending our knowledge of what is happening now. In the eyes of most corporate "survivors," management plans for reorganization and reengineering have resulted in fewer jobs or in more work being done with the same number of people—a process that is rapidly spreading to government agencies, educational institutions, and even to smaller firms.

Collapsing Job Ladders

One of the ways in which reengineering results in downsizing is through collapsing job ladders and/or pulling titles out of use, so that workers will assume more functions and be more "flexible." This type of corporate delayering affects everyone. It not only changes the labor process (the way work is done), but also effects the labor market, because it results in fewer entry-level positions for people coming into office jobs and fewer opportunities for moving up.

In the years of economic expansion following World War II, job ladders were part of what economists call an *internal labor market.* Job ladders provided a well-marked, bureaucratic career path within a company that offered the chance for promotion and acknowledged that on-the-job training was necessary to move from one rung to the next—from trainee up through junior, senior, associate, and so on. For people who had made it inside these organizational walls, internal labor markets were both a form of security and a way to think about *careers* rather than just jobs.

Job ladders had a negative side, however. They worked relatively well for white college-educated men in organizations where the ladder progressed up through middle management. They were less effective for white college-educated women who—depending on luck (of department or boss)—might make it to the professional ranks but then faced a "glass ceiling" somewhere around lower middle management; and they were even less effective for white women who came in through the clerical route, where ladders tended to end with the title of office manager.

For minority men and women, particularly those entering through the mailroom or back-office clerical departments, career ladders were almost nonexistent. The Civil Rights Act of 1963 and the equal opportunity and affirmative action policies of the 1970s helped, but gaining a toehold on the corporate ladder has remained extremely difficult. (While government offices, particularly municipal agencies, were more open to people of color, government jobs are notorious for their dead-end ladders.) A clerk-typist, for example, might make it to word-processor but there the ladder stopped. Similarly, a mailroom clerk might switch to the copy center, but he or she had little chance of moving out of the support area. In other words, for most of the period that job ladders and internal labor markets dominated the organizational landscape, white skin, a college degree, and some sort of middle-class belief in bureaucratic rules were necessary to move beyond the lowest rungs.

Elastic (Broad)bands

As part of the reengineering process, job ladders are now being replaced by different sorts of "broad banding," clumping jobs into bands that involve a wide range of presumably interchangeable skills and operational responsibilities, like the bands in Jack's large firm, or those we saw in Chapter 1 in Glenda's administrative job with a telecommunications company.

Broad banding works something like this: people within a band—for example, administrative support—are expected to assume responsibility for a greater number of tasks and for more work. Working in teams, so that any worker can fill in for any other worker, often accompanies broad banding. It is generally assumed that this flexibility increases productivity, and, as anecdotal evidence indicates, most office workers feel that they are producing more, as do the companies they work for. A vice-president of human resources for a large bank explained it to me this way: "The bottom line is that there are no straight ladders anymore. Employees need to figure out what path they can take and get the skills to do more and prove that they are responsible for doing more. Lateral moves are what they should be looking for."

There is a double standard at work in the creation of teams and broad bands. On the one hand, managers are told to invest in people; on the other hand, they are told to cut out as many people as possible. Business magazines emphasize human potential and building what is called "human capital"—arguing that people can be expected to increase their "worth" through skills and training. A typical example, written in the trendy tone of *Forbes* magazine, states: "Winners [companies] in the Information Age will be evident by their supreme ability to liberate human creativity, create customized products, streamline distribution, get closer to the customer, and cut costs."[5] Like so much we hear, this reiterates the key phrases that Michael Hammer and other gurus of reengineering use in their doctoring effort to sugar-coat the often bitter bill of reengineered jobs.

Job bands may, in theory, "liberate" creativity by giving people room to do more and different tasks (if this is in fact a form of liberation), but their true purpose is to cut costs. And cutting costs generally limits the number of jobs and therefore the opportunities for promotion. And when occupational bands are

An executive on the road, 1994. Using his company-issued laptop with modem, and talking on his portable phone, he gets on-line—in a hotel kitchen—in order to check his email. [Andy Freeberg]

used in conjunction with longer periods between salary reviews and coupled with the use of temps who work side-by-side with full-time employees, they are reminders to full-time employees that they may be only one step away from temporary status.

SKILLS, SKILLS, AND MORE SKILLS

By most accounts, work reorganization and information technology are together increasing management's expectations of what office workers can and should do. As the vice-president of a large organization put it, "The bar has been raised"—meaning that more and more is expected of new entrants and longer time workers in the intensified office environment. Yet there are still ongoing debates about which "skills" are really in demand, and indeed about what the concept of skill actually includes. Collapsing job ladders and banding together titles and functions has broadened job content and skill ranges for most jobs. Team work and flatter organizational structures reinforce the fact that workers and tasks are highly *interdependent,* with workers depending on others for getting higher volumes of work done. And this interdependence of tasks and workers is locked into the reengineering process and the technology that supports it.

The deskilling debates of the 1970s and the upskilling arguments of the 1980s often talked past each other because they were looking at different characteristics of the complex concept that we call skill. Certainly skill includes *individual attributes* (like being "good with people"), *job characteristics* (like using computer applications), and *power relationships* (such as belonging to an occupational group that is recognized and remunerated for its skills).[6] While it is clear that more office workers are expected to have a broader *range* of skills in each of these categories, the focus has also been on the need for all office staff to be familiar with standard computer applications.

It is now beginning to be recognized that so-called personal attributes, like "interpersonal and communication skills," are essential for getting the work done, although many people have argued that these attributes have always been important invisible skills in clerical work.[7] In the following examples, we will see that managers have high expectations for aspects of skill that include individual attributes and job characteristics, but that jobs that do not have professional status—and thus power—are not adequately compensated for the rise in expectations.

Take telephone operations, for example. In the 1970s and 1980s, this work became so routinized that much of it is now "plugged" into computer software. Yet operators continue to use a wide range of skills, including decision-making and complex reasoning. Cecilia, a bilingual (Spanish-English) telephone operator, is called upon to use just such a range of skills when she plugs into the supposedly user-friendly computer system.

According to her procedures manual, Cecilia is supposed to enter the first four letters of a primary search key for each directory assistance inquiry she receives. The rules state that for business calls, she is to enter the first significant word in the title of the business; for residence inquiries, the first four characters of the person's last name; and for government information, the first important word in the lowest level of the applicable agency.

But it often doesn't work according to the rules. In southern California, for example, simply entering "Hern" for Hernández would bring forth so many names that she would have to spend more time on the call than she is allotted, so she asks about maternal and paternal family names in order to narrow the search. In addition, callers often don't know the exact address of the person they are looking for but only the neighborhoods, which Cecilia too has to know so that she can search in the right database. Business calls are even more complicated, because many businesses are listed under the first name of the proprietor—like *Charlie* Anderson's restaurant—while doctors and lawyers are listed by *last* name. Some callers have limited proficiency in English, so whenever possible she switches into Spanish, but in other cases she has to listen very carefully and try to coach the caller, using "tricks" she has learned after several years on the job.

Despite Cecilia's skills and experience, she is one of tens of thousands of operators who are worried that their jobs will be cut as part of massive layoffs in telephone companies across the country. To make matters worse, Cecilia works for a nonunion long-distance carrier, so she has no job security—not even seniority—to rely on.

We turn now to the work of an editorial assistant, where we can again see a clear pattern of increasing computer-based skills as well as a wider range of responsibilities. In one sense this work is another example of the "professionalization" of clerical work, as many editorial assistants have taken on more professional tasks, while some of the more tedious clerical work has been absorbed into computer-based systems. Here is Joyce's story as she told it to me when I interviewed her a year ago.

Joyce is a senior editorial assistant, having just been promoted to senior level after only a year with the publishing firm. Like most of her co-workers, she has a degree in English and, after a "fair amount of temping," is glad to be working in a field related to her interests.

"My editor is self-sufficient," she says. "She types her own letters and does most of her own correspondence." Joyce does "tons of photocopying," sends out manuscripts, writes her own letters to authors, and handles the volumes of paper involved in getting a book from manuscript through to publication. She is comfortable using a variety of word-processing and some graphics programs and the company's custom-made "pre-publication" system, but she is "alarmed by how much time she sits staring at the computer." She won't say how much she earns since it is against company rules to talk about salary, but in "ballpark" figures she makes roughly a third of what editors make.

Joyce has since left the publishing job and is working as an administrative assistant/office manager for an academic department in a university. While she liked the professional responsibility of editorial work, she couldn't get by on the $17,500 she was making at the publishing firm. Although she never planned on a clerical or administrative career, the tight labor market has squeezed her out of other positions, and like many college graduates she continues to gravitate toward work that at least lets her think for herself. In this sense, the so-called professionalization of clerical work means that while clerical salaries don't hold a candle to professional ones, workers like

Darleen and Joyce don't have to follow pre-scripted and pre-rationalized procedures.

Meanwhile, at the professional end of broad-banded occupations, many professionals below top-level managers have learned to handle most of their own clerical work. An example is Robert, an executive editor at a university press. He transferred to the New York office at a time when a new computer and phone system had just been installed. Both were initially strange to him, as was the fact that there were no secretaries in the office.

Robert has a corner cubicle, with fabric-covered walls that run three-quarters of the way to the ceiling. I interviewed him only a few months after, as he put it, "the computer system was plunked down on my desk." He wasn't hostile toward the computer itself, but felt that "as a two-finger typist" he needed more training and practice. Other than a half-day training session, he has been left to "learn the computer" on his own.

While he was not initially pleased to be doing his own word-processing, he suspects that the time it takes to send out a letter is about the same as when he gave his handwritten notes to his secretary. "Before," he explains, "I gave something to my secretary, and depending on what else she was doing, or whatever questions she had for me, she gave it back to me and I had to proofread it later. Now I can write and proofread something while I am still thinking about it." But the upshot is that he is taking more work home, and, in the new organization of things, he is responsible for producing more books.

Cecilia's job as a telephone operator is in the "high-tech" telecommunications industry. It also represents a "high-skill" occupation. In government and academic terms, it is part of the "high performance workplace" in that a variety of skills, technology, and a reengineered work process have led to more output per worker.[8] But there the string of "highs" stops, for Cecilia's job is not high-wage; nor does it include even a moderate degree of security. Joyce's editorial jobs come closer to fulfilling the "high-tech–high-skill–high performance" scenario, particularly with its professionalization of clerical tasks, but the picture is flawed again by the low wages editorial assistants earn. Robert never chose his career expecting it to be part of a high-tech, high-performance scenario, yet the "clericalization of professional work" has also placed him squarely in front of a computer. As a professional, however, Robert has the advantage of the traditional power relations of skill—he is compensated for the range and variety of skills he uses, although his salary has not increased to correspond with the amount of clerical work he is doing, or to compensate him for the fact that he is expected to take on the production of additional books.

In the 1980s it was argued that high-tech, high-skill jobs would be the winners in the new information age, particularly in terms of compensating workers for their acquired computer skills. But as the above situations show, there is little evidence to support this. When we look at other occupations, we see a similar picture. Teller and platform people (customer representatives) in banks, having learned several computer systems, have not seen their new skills reflected in their paychecks. The pattern is repeated for insurance claims processors, who do almost all their work on computers. Similarly, the salaries of airline reservation clerks and most customer service representatives do not reflect their newly acquired computer-based skills.[9]

In the reengineered workplace, workers can have as many skills as they need to get the job done and as they have time to learn, but management has increasingly divorced compensation from skill. This is the same pattern that low-waged clerical work is known for: skills like on-the-job knowledge, the ability to set priorities, draw up schedules, and make decisions have long been invisible in the cost accounting of the clerical worker's paycheck.[10] It should come as no surprise that the political and power-based strategy used in undervaluing women's work—an extremely cost-effective one—is now being applied to jobs held by men.

We have seen how reengineering and skill expectations have altered the workplace. It is now time to take a look at how technology fits into this scenario.

NETWORKED!

Networks are as central to the 1990s as personal computers were to the 1980s. By 1994, 87 percent of large firms and 32 percent of smaller companies had some form of Local Area Network (LAN).[11] And increasing number of organizations have also installed Wide Area Networks (WANs), which link computers in different departments, buildings, and cities. And probably the most dominant feature of today's workplace is the fact that individuals and organizations are more easily hooked into worldwide networks, like the Internet, joining what the media likes to call the "information superhighway."

Networks were a technical development waiting to happen. In the 1980s, we saw how users, managers, and systems analysts were frustrated by the lack of compatible software and what technicians call standard "protocols," which allow information sent from one computer—either via modem or through a local network—to be received on another computer (or fax machine). By the mid-1990s, agreements between hardware and software companies, along with industry-wide standards, smoothed out the majority of pre-existing hardware and software problems. These weren't in any case so much technical problems as situations that required companies and the government to sit down and hammer out standards that they could all adhere to. The standards then gave companies room to carve out their market niches.

Setting such network standards fit in well with plans to remove middle managers and incorporate the information and reports they had once generated directly into databases that could be brought up on different computer screens, whenever and wherever they were needed. Network standards also fit in with reengineering plans that called for abolishing lower level tasks like

Speaking the Language of Network Protocol

Artificial Intelligence (AI) Software that is supposed to solve problems in the same way people solve them, although most AI assumes rule-based "behavior," and human intelligence most often involves breaking rules.

Client-server Networks that are distributed directly to the user's computer via file servers—as in "we" are the clients and the computer is our "server."

Communications (Tele) or distance links between computers. The term used to mean what we did in a "face-to-face" way (see below).

Face-to-face F2F in email language. People actually communicating with each other; not virtual communication.

Information (Super) Highway The worldwide network of networks linking computers, faxes, phones, videos, CD-ROMs, and any form of digital "communication."

Master-slave The mainframe networks in the old days: the mainframe was the "master" and the terminals were its "slaves"—the opposite of the client-server systems.

Motherboard The main circuit board (literally a board) that the other parts of a computer plug in to. It's interesting that there are not that many female terms applied to computer parts, yet this one is the "mother" of them all.

Network Anything that is linked together to send and receive messages. In the 1980s, "networking" generally referred to social groups and to the activities of job hunters.

Protocol A standardized set of procedures that facilitates links between one system and another—a sort of diplomacy among computers.

data entry and repackaging them into integrated jobs—like Sandy's position as a customer service rep with a bank's telephone service operation.

Meanwhile, telephone and cable companies, television studios, and media mega-corporations are positioning themselves to install fiber optic cables—long thin strands of glass fiber that are the building blocks needed to transmit hundreds of thousands of data communications simultaneously. Fiber optics have been around for several decades, but it was not until the 1990s that demand for its use grew. This demand is in part created by the higher volume of business transactions now being carried out over distances, and in part by the increase in the type of digital communications taking place. For instance, in the 1980s, businesses were content to fax documents from one place to another; now multi-media transactions—including video clips, long data files, color photographs, graphics, documents, and electronic messages (email)—are becoming the norm, drastically increasing the volume of information flowing through networks.

Computer jargon seems to be expanding at an exponential rate, but there is a common thread holding much of it together. Most of the terms take on a kind of anthropomorphism—setting human terms onto technical ones, perhaps in the belief that we will not fight change if we feel "at home" with the words used to describe it. The box on the facing page gives some of the technical terms with human characteristics that are being used today.

Networks also support organizations that want to divide their labor force geographically and get more output from the same number of workers—or, where possible, fewer workers. This is still another aspect of reengineering: moving people, offices, and functions around in an attempt to lower real estate and salary costs. According to the chief technology officer for Chase Manhattan Bank, networks increase productivity by increasing the amount that can be processed at any one time. Chase, for example, had 100 data-processing centers in the United States and Europe; now there are only two, one in London and one in New

York. Both operate with a fraction of the former workforce, and when one center has too much processing, the overflow is switched across the Atlantic.[12] Investment in more reliable and standardized hardware and software, along with access to leased network lines, makes it possible for management to cut payrolls and provides the flexibility to keep them cut.[13]

STRESS AND WORK ENVIRONMENT ISSUES

There is no question that the pulse of office life is running faster. Sometimes the computer speeds up the pace, sometimes the fax, sometimes voice mail, but most often it is the way the work has been organized so that fewer people will produce more. Whether this is called efficiency, productivity, or simply speed-up, there are few office occupations where workers do not feel the push to work faster and longer, and to do more.

The quickened pace of office work intensifies physical problems that were first noticed in the 1980s, when computer use was expanding. Growing bodies of evidence show that injuries from repetitive use of the keyboard—commonly called Repetitive Strain Injuries (RSI)—account for at least 60 percent of all workplace injuries. Journalists were among the first to sue their employers because of these problems, particularly tenosynovitis and carpel tunnel syndrome, which come from prolonged rapid use of the keyboard. To avoid these serious problems, workers should not sit at the computer for more than two hours at a time, or for more than twenty hours a week.[14] Yet jobs like customer service representative are *designed* for people to sit in one place and remain at the keyboard for four hours or more, with only short breaks in between.

And while repetitive strain injuries have made it into the headlines, the radiation hazard from the computer monitor is not as frequently discussed. Low-level radiation from monitors is directly linked to severe headaches and to cellular damage, possibly including cancers. Radiation hazards drop off for people sitting at least an arm's length away from the screen, but many people lean closer, and at distances of less than 2 feet electro-magnetic emissions rise rapidly. Electromagnetic radiation from the back of the screen is even higher, which creates problems in poorly designed offices where computers are placed back to back. In addition, the monitors' bright reflective screens can cause a range of serious eye problems.[15]

In ergonomic terms, none of these problems is insurmountable. European countries, for example, have set manufacturing standards for monitors and keyboards that lessen the risks. Similarly, many northern European countries have adopted legislation that redesigns jobs so that workers don't have to be in front of computers for longer than recommended time periods. But currently, more and more Americans are spending longer and longer hours sitting in front of computers in jobs that have been designed—and even reengineered—to ignore these health risks.

A TALE OF (AT LEAST) TWO WORKFORCES

Job restructuring has gradually polarized the workforce across the United States, making the gap between rich and poor more noticeable, and, as noted earlier, putting fear into the hearts of those who have managed to hang onto their jobs. In 1994, the gap between rich and poor was the widest since the Census Bureau started tracking income in 1947: the top fifth of all households took in 44.6 percent of all income, while the bottom fifth took in only 4.4 percent.[16] White-collar workers are still more likely to be in the top half of income brackets, but many are learning that the color of their collar is no guarantee that they will stay there.

Bob Hall, an analyst with the Institute for Southern Studies, describes this polarized situation:

> The South, like the rest of the nation, is developing a two-track economy, two-track workforce, and two-track lifestyle. There are more B.M.W.s in the South, and there are more mobile homes,

and these days there's a sense of anxiety among ordinary working people that's almost palpable.[17]

The two-tiered, two-track workforce Hall writes about is not confined to the South. Indeed, reengineering, downsizing, outsourcing, and a full range of office technology have not only been used to widen the gap between rich and poor, but have divided the workforce into *four* tracks. The top tier includes professional and managerial workers in payroll or employer-based jobs; they earn relatively high salaries and have more stable working situations. Jack, the programming manager, and Robert, the senior editor, have these kinds of jobs. The second tier includes lower waged workers who are closer to losing their regular pay checks and benefits. Cecilia's job with the telephone company fits this pattern, as does Sheila's word-processing work (discussed in Chapter 1). Many of these jobs are in administrative support positions, but growing numbers are technical and supervisory.

These two tiers of payroll positions are held in place by a third track, or tier, made up of contingent workers, and by a fourth—unemployed people. Contingent workers are those who have no fixed position within an organization: they may be part-timers, temps on short-term assignments, leased employees, independent contractors, and subcontractors, as well as people trying to start their own businesses. The majority have no employment agreement and work either for a temporary help agency or as some form of independent freelancer.

It is generally estimated that at least one out of four workers in the United States is a contingent or supplemental worker— roughly 28 percent of the workforce. While it is difficult to find reliable data on supplemental workers, it is generally accepted that about 39 million Americans were "contingent" or supplemental workers in 1993, and that in the same period there were somewhere around 21 million part-time workers.[18] A director of Human Resources for a large computer company told me that his company was planning for more than 50 percent of its workforce to be supplemental workers. "They are like a renewable

resource," he explained, "there when you need them and gone when you don't; and all without having to pay benefits."

Unlike prior cycles of economic downturn and business expansion, economic growth in the mid-1990s is not bringing back payroll jobs. As the chairman of a large advertising agency explained, "It is not as necessary to add people to the payroll as business improves because of all the freelance art directors, copywriters, and the like out there."[19]

Getting by in the 1990s has meant that more people within a household are pooling their resources. Barbara Presley Noble, the author of the "At Work" column in the *New York Times* business section, has put it this way:

> American households have coped with the decline in real wages and the erosion of their standard of living by putting more able bodies—mostly women—to work, taking on second and third jobs or acceding to the labor market and accepting temporary, contingent and lower wage work.[20]

What is particularly noticeable is the increasing and steady presence of married women and mothers in the labor force. Somewhere around 15 million working wives keep their families in the top income tier by holding comparatively well paying professional and executive jobs. But *New York Times* reporter Peter Kilborn noted that "far more—37 million—are working for lower wages as clerks and cashiers, nurses' aides and bank tellers, secretaries and maids. Their wages serve as a cushion between welfare and getting by."[21] And most common is the presence of multiple job holders in one household, people who work a part-time job in addition to a full-time one, and those who have to string several part-time jobs together. The Bureau of Labor Statistics reported that in February 1994 there were at least 7 million multiple job holders in the United States, and that 47 percent of them were women.[22]

There is an often repeated story that is said to have taken place in a General Motors plant in 1955. Walter Reuther, president of the United Auto Workers union, was touring the plant with Charles Wilson, its chief executive officer (later to become Eisenhower's Secretary of Defense). Wilson, referring to plans to automate the plant, asked Reuther who would pay union dues. Reuther replied, "Who's going to buy your cars?"[23] The question remains appropriate today. Work reorganization, job redesign, and skill changes have brought about a growing gap between rich and poor and challenged a number of fundamental assumptions about the links among hard work, pay, and some form of job security. Households in the bottom quarter of income levels earned an average of $11,530 in 1992, nowhere near enough to buy the products and services of the industries they work in. And while those in the top 25 percent are comparatively well off with average incomes of $91,368,[24] the growing spread of insecurity propelled by the uncoupling of skill and pay, and jobs and career tracks, could put longer term economic growth in question.

6

THE OFFICE OF THE FUTURE MAY BE HOME

"We have fewer people doing much more work, much of which is knowledge-based, and we're paying people less."

—CEO, 1994[1]

In 1994, the cover story of an issue of *Fortune* magazine proclaimed "The End of the Job." The author argued that traditional employment in well-worn occupational categories was "no longer the best way to organize work," and that the traditional job was becoming a "social artifact."[2] *Business Week* claims that there is a surge in the number of workers being pushed out by waves of downsizing, forming a large pool of what it calls "corporate refugees." In the spring of 1993, the magazine said that there were over 2 million such corporate refugees, most of whom had been laid off from well-paying managerial positions. In November 1993, *Time* magazine—speaking to a more general audience—wrote that "By now, these trends have created an 'industrial reserve army'—to borrow a term from Karl Marx—so large that a quite extraordinary and prolonged surge in output would be required to put all its members to full-time, well-paid work." According to *Time,* "The white-collar layoffs are permanent and structural. These jobs are gone forever."[3]

The TV and radio talk-show culture pushes the myth of high-tech, high-skill, high-wage jobs in its one-minute soundbites. Yet, as we saw in the last chapter, more and more categories of office-based jobs do not fit into this optimistic scenario. Here we turn to work that has, through reengineering, downsizing, outsourcing, and networked information technology, "been shoved outside the security blanket of big companies," and made into contingent work.[4] We will also take a look at jobs that are disappearing altogether.

CONTINGENT WORK—A TEMPORARY CONDITION?

Look in any "Help Wanted" section of the newspaper and you will see a large number of ads for temporary help placement agencies. These agencies, which are part of the business services industry, place almost 2 million workers in any given month.[5] In fact, Manpower, Inc., the largest temp or staffing agency in the United States, is also the largest private employer, with a payroll of 600,000 workers—four times as large as the domestic payrolls of either IBM or Ford.[6] In 1994, the three fastest growing U.S. industries were business services, health care, and social services.[7] The business services industry, the only one of the three that applies specifically to office work, is made up of the firms that supply temporary or supplemental workers to other companies.

A president of one large temporary placement agency in New York told me that temp agencies prefer the term "staffing services" to "temporary services," because assignments last anywhere from one day to six months or more. Her company has been around for over twenty-five years and has gone from placing mostly clerical or back-office support staff to handling a full range of occupations, from interim management to doctors, lawyers, and accountants—all on a temporary basis—as well as offering executive search services. "Companies downsized or 'rightsized,' as they call it," she explains, "and then realized that they were stretched so thin that they needed someone to get a department up and running." Meanwhile, the real profit center of her business is project-based occupations that need people like architects, engineers, and computer programmers for projects that last for a specific length of time.

Staffing assignments that last longer than one year are generally called "employee leasing," and this too is a growing area. One temporary CEO pointed out the advantage to the corporation of having high-level temps: "There can be real value in having a throwaway executive," he said, "one who can come in and do unpleasant, nasty things like kill off a few sacred cows."[8] As the CEO of an executive search firm noted, "We always hunted heads; now we simply sell *and* rent them."[9]

Until recently most work that was outsourced was undertaken by smaller subcontractors who specialized in servicing back-office operations for such operations as banks or computer centers. Now there are many variations on this theme, including some large companies that are starting their own outsourcing firms. Xerox, for example, is not only outsourcing staff jobs but has at the same time set up a subsidiary to provide mailrooms and print shops for other firms, and AT&T has done the same, specializing in the telecommunications operations that are being outsourced by banks.[10] Company functions that were once considered essential "in-house" services, immune from outsourcing, are increasingly being delegated to subsidiaries or outsourcing companies. American Airlines, for example, has outsourced its customer service operations at thirty airports, and one large bank has farmed out work formerly done by its internal auditing department.[11] These decisions are generally presented in terms of the balance sheet: outsourced firms and subsidiaries lower payroll expenses and cut the cost of benefits and the costs of letting employees go the next time business slows down.

Sending work to subsidiaries isn't limited to outsourcing firms in the United States. For instance, the high-tech "knowledge work" of developing computer software is a growing industry overseas. By using networks to send the resulting software "product" back, U.S. companies can hire highly skilled programmers in Russia, the Czech Republic, and India at a fraction of what they would cost in the United States.

For those who have been pushed outside of corporate walls, the result has been less economic security and a great deal of stress. For example, one chemical engineer who lost his job in the aerospace industry spent months sending out hundreds of resumes and finding nothing that resembled full-time permanent employment. He says that "most companies didn't even bother to answer" his resume blitz, and that he was forced to "eat up" his savings. A temporary placement agency that specializes in engineering and scientific jobs finally found him a one-month assignment analyzing potable water and hazardous waste on the evening shift at the subsidiary of a larger company. Like many short-term temps, he has managed to extend his assignment over several months. While the job offers no benefits, he is now earning the $35,000 he made before, although he gets this only by working six to eight hours overtime each week.[12] This is not exactly the high-wage, secure work that engineering was supposed to be.

All these changes are part of a growing pattern of shifting financial risk from large organizations to smaller ones, and from management to the individual worker.[13] In the 1980s, management talked of needing "just-in-time" products in order to compete in the global market. Now, in addition to flexible product inventories, employees too have become a "just-in-time" variable. Originally "just in time" meant that parts and products would be produced as they were needed, thus reducing the expense of keeping inventories. In the world of office work,

A home office, 1995. This researcher, who works on a contract basis, does most of her writng at night. She schedules trips into the main office once or twice a week. [Les Leopold]

"just-in-time" workers are those drawn from the contingent workforce: companies lower their costs by not keeping people on the payroll, hiring them only during peak periods or times of expanding output. This has many advantages for the firm but comparatively few for the worker.

Some of this reorganization has been borrowed (somewhat loosely) from Japanese management strategies, which caught the interest of U.S. managers in the early 1980s. For instance, automakers in Japan assemble cars, but the majority of parts are made by smaller subcontracting firms whose "peripheral" workers can be called in as needed. This has led to a two-tiered workforce: core employees with the "parent" firm and peripheral workers in the subcontracting firms, each with different pay scales and job titles. Core workers are in effect permanent employees, and until recently had something close to jobs for life in exchange for their dedication and loyalty to the company. Peripheral workers, on the other hand, are part of what economists call the secondary labor market, with their job security and wages dependent on the sales of the subcontractor's product and the number of other peripheral workers competing for their jobs. It has been a successful system for producing low-priced cars, but it is a brutal way to treat workers in the labor market.

In the United States, the creation of a "just-in-time" production process has gone one step further and been applied throughout the white-collar sector. Here parent companies squeeze competitive prices out of subcontractors, who in turn squeeze lower priced contracts out of the large reserve pool of individual freelancers, many of whom are willing to take whatever comes along to pay the bills.

FALSE ASSUMPTIONS

Until recently it was assumed by both management consultants and economists that women made up most of the contingent and part-time workforce because they were the ones who needed flexible work schedules to fit with child care, school, and other needs. In other words, it was assumed that the contingent workforce was made up of women who wanted it to be that way.

It is hard to know if this was ever true, but it certainly is not true today. Eileen Appelbaum summarizes a series of studies of contingent work this way: "The results ... suggest that women are taking the growing number of temp agency jobs because employers are creating more temporary positions in the fields where women typically work, and not because temporary employment better meets their flexibility needs."[14] The same is true for part-time work. Twenty-seven percent of women workers work part time, but, as Chris Tilly notes, "While women are more likely to *choose* part-time work, they are also more likely to be *stuck* in part-time jobs against their will."[15] And people who work part time often work at several jobs to make ends meet.

Working part-time and having to combine several jobs is even more the case for black workers, who are already heavily concentrated in lower paying positions. Clearly neither part-time nor contingency work meets the need for economic security, family health benefits, pensions, or promotion. These issues form the dividing line between core and peripheral status. Bureau of Labor Statistics figures show how much part-time work is involuntary: in 1994, there were between 4.4 and 6.2 million part-time workers who were actively looking for full-time work.[16]

As with other dividing lines, professional women find it easier to combine part-time and temporary work with child care than do clerical workers. Professional workers not only earn a great deal more in the hours they work, but they also have more control over arranging when they work. For example, a lawyer who gets assignments from Attorneys Per Diem, a Baltimore-based legal temp firm, says, "I don't have to look over my shoulder when I have three pediatrician appointments in a row. And I don't have to answer to anyone if I have only three billable hours in one day."[17] On the other side of the divide, temp workers in clerical positions generally rely almost entirely on this income. While these jobs sometimes offer "flexibility"—for instance, night or evening shift work—they do not offer the choice of hours or working conditions that professional jobs do.

VIRTUAL CORPORATIONS–VIRTUAL OFFICES

According to current management literature, to be competitive, today's companies must become "virtual corporations." Virtual corporations spread their operations out, maintaining only a skeletal staff at headquarters and outsourcing or contracting out many jobs and functions. They are linked through "virtual offices" as individual employees—temporary or otherwise—are increasingly encouraged to "telecommute." This means that they work from home via a computer or that they work in smaller satellite centers where groups of firms, small and large, share office space. One estimate put the number of telecommuters at 6.6 million in 1993,[18] but since the Los Angeles earthquake in early 1994, and in accordance with new guidelines to lessen air pollution through car-pools and "other means," management journals have been raving about telecommuting via the information superhighway.

Reengineered work processes, backed up by telecommunication and computer networks, make these kinds of smaller, spread-out organizational settings increasingly possible. In 1994, for instance, IBM set up a "virtual office" in New Jersey, accompanied by a great deal of publicity and with an eye toward making significant cuts in its expenses for office space. The company collapsed five branch offices and sent sales and systems people out into the field with portable computers and mobile communications. The office is a warehouse filled with small cubicles that have connections for computers and telephones. The cubicles are shared—people are assigned to them as they come in, much like the rotating office space used in Peggy's advertising agency, described in the first chapter.

In the beginning of the 1990s, before virtual offices came along, middle managers in many companies were skeptical about telecommuting and other forms of remote work because they were concerned that without supervision office workers wouldn't perform. But by mid-decade top managers were strongly advocating these moves and middle managers were finding that productivity among those working outside the office had risen. Studies have also shown that direct supervision no longer appears to be a major issue in getting workers to produce more.[19] Among other factors, the fact that more and more project-based work has deadlines, coupled with rising job insecurity in general, means that former office-based workers—from clericals through the professional ranks—are pushing themselves harder and working longer hours.[20]

IBM's virtual office building in New Jersey, 1994. This 100,000-square-foot former warehouse contains 400 desks that are assigned to salespeople who have no permanent offices. [© 1994 Tim Redel]

Software designed as "groupware" makes it easier for professionals and administrative support workers to share documents and files, and it also makes it easier for companies to justify the fact that work can be spread over time and space in the shapeless form of the virtual office. Yet even advocates of the virtual office admit that one of its problems is that there is no "virtual watercooler"—no place where workers meet to chat and to exchange ideas and solve problems that have to do with their work.

DISAPPEARING JOBS AND FALLING WAGES

The media has been giving big play to stories about cuts in middle level and professional jobs, but this type of compression has been going on in clerical and back-office jobs for a while. The story of Roger, the insurance policy assembler described in Chapter 1, helps us understand the powerful interplay of management policies that reorganize work and introduce technology in order to reduce the workforce. Here is how the story continues:

According to Roger, his company's restructuring was accompanied by a great deal of fanfare. "I had a promising job in a company that said it was becoming leaner (smaller), healthier (more profitable), and meaner (more competitive). Then a new computer system was introduced, and we suddenly saw the consolidation of service offices scattered across the country into bigger regional centers to form a critical mass needed to satisfy the new [computer] system's needs. There was talk of restructuring. New opportunities. The future lies ahead. Banners were run up. White ones said 'quality' or 'service'; black ones 'global competition' and 'economic downturn.'"[21]

But Roger's job, like the jobs of over 200 clerical workers in the division he worked for, was wiped out by the consolidation of services and the new computer system. Such tales can be told of other industries. Banks, for example, got rid of 179,000 tellers between 1983 and 1993.[22] The computer system at Roger's company was custom-designed to take over minutely divided work tasks, called "work units," and build them into the computer software. In the 1970s and 1980s, most insurance firms and banks tried automated systems like this, but they had only limited success in actually eliminating jobs. From the company's perspective, this was because work tasks were not sufficiently isolated, the workforce of full-timers had more power to do the work as it saw fit, and the computer software wasn't designed to take into account the variety of tasks to be done. In the 1990s, after some years of reorganization and computerization, systems like the one introduced at Roger's insurance company, combined with organizational restructuring, replaced not only tasks but entire job categories.

The effects of the restructuring of work are clearly visible throughout the administrative support area, where a number of jobs have simply disappeared. For example, keypunch operators had been phased out by the end of the 1980s, along with teletype operators and type compositors in the printing industry. In the 1990s, there has been a sustained decline of key administrative support (clerical) job categories. According to the Bureau of Labor Statistics, administrative support, including clerical work, is still the largest occupational group, but by 1994 there were 2.6 million secretaries, down from 3.1 million in 1983. On the other hand, there was an increase in the number of information clerks, but over half of these are receptionists. In 1994, information clerks were earning on average only $322 a week, markedly below the secretarial median wage of $383.[23] Thus while we know from anecdotal experience that some secretaries have moved up to more administrative computer-concentrated positions, the general trend is a decline in the large and relatively low-paying secretarial category and an increase in the extremely low-paying information clerk category. In addition, as companies rely more and more on voice mail and electronic mail, the job of receptionist is also beginning to decline. This is fostered by security concerns: as offices are increasingly turned into locked corridors and closed-off areas, security guards are more likely than receptionists to be the ones who greet visitors.

Telephone operators, a job that once provided a bridge to better work for many women, has declined by 50,000 jobs since 1990, leaving only 120,000 operators in payroll jobs in 1994. But in early 1994, AT&T announced plans to cut back to fewer than 10,000 operators within the next year. Other telephone companies are following suit, cutting office staff, directory assistance personnel, and installation and repair workers. In January 1994, for example, NYNEX, the large New York-based phone company, announced plans to cut 22 percent of its workforce, or

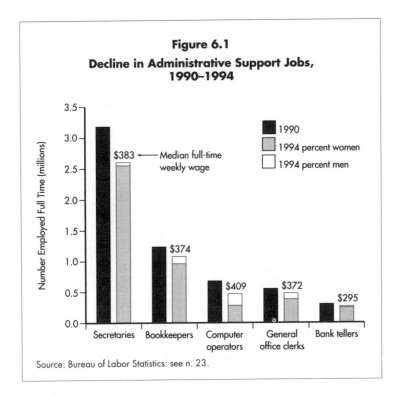

Figure 6.1

Decline in Administrative Support Jobs, 1990–1994

Source: Bureau of Labor Statistics: see n. 23.

almost 17,000 workers. The company had already cut 13,000 jobs during the previous four years.[24]

Financial records processing, with little more than 1.4 million workers—once the backbone of back-office work—has also begun to decline. Between 1990 and 1994, this area lost 208,000 workers. Even greater decreases can be expected to result from the combined pressures of automating entire aspects of some jobs, such as check processing, outsourcing other parts to areas with cheaper labor, and using temps to fill in when needed.[25]

While administrative support and back-office jobs experienced the first cuts, positions that are now being slashed are further up the organizational ladder. There has been a slow but steady chipping away at professional and technical jobs, and supervisors through mid-level managers have been hard pressed in the last few years. Temporary help agencies report that laid-off managers, particularly men in their fifties, are having a very difficult time finding anything resembling permanent work. Indeed, according to the American Association of Retired Persons (AARP), in 1994 there were at least 12 organizations with 9,000 members that had been organized to fight companies and help people in their forties and fifties who had been downsized out of a job.[26]

Some supposedly high-tech professional jobs like electrical and electronic engineering have also been declining—precisely the areas that were supposed to be boosted by the growth of Silicon Valley industries and the associated rise of PCs and telecommunications. The number of aerospace engineers, for example, went from 104,000 full-time positions in 1990 to 73,000 in 1994, while electrical and electronic engineers went down from 568,000 to 526,000 in the same period.[27]

The number of computer programming jobs declined by 49,000 between 1990 and 1994, the result of the move to off-the-shelf applications as well as outsourcing to other countries. Since government projections proclaim this as a growing field, it is important to note that the entire occupational category included only 495,000 full-time workers in 1994—a mid-ranged occupational category when compared to over 1.2 million accountants or 2.6 million secretaries.

IF THE ANSWER IS EDUCATION, WHAT IS THE QUESTION?

By most accounts, falling into the bottom of the tracked economy is the fault of the worker—for not getting enough education or for failing to learn the right skills—a sophisticated way of continuing to "blame the victim." It is a fact that college graduates earn more over their lifetimes than high school graduates, and that high school graduates have a hard time finding anything other than what one observer has called minimum-wage

"MacJobs." Yet this does not speak to the specifics of what is happening to college graduates today; nor does it address the complexity and costliness of accumulating skills that are outdated within a few years.

More and more people are going to college now, yet the bachelors' degree no longer provides an automatic ticket to a middle-class job. As the *Arizona Republic* reported in 1994, "Although there are no firm statistics, placement officials fear that 30 to 40 percent of college graduates are taking jobs that don't require degrees."[28] Applications to graduate school are up sharply as undergraduates find that competition has brought about "degree inflation." In a job market where there are many applicants for each position, employers can pick and choose, honing in on those with the most education and emphasizing previous on-the-job experience. As one recent graduate said to me, "How can I get an entry level job that requires a minimum of two years prior experience?"

A study conducted for the University of Delaware showed that the average salary for its college graduates, $24,385 in 1994, was the lowest in fifteen years. Business majors, who many people expect to earn more than others, are having a hard time because there are more of them than the number of jobs available. The College Placement Council in Bethlehem, Pennsylvania, for example, reported that the starting salaries of business majors averaged only $23,820 last year. And fields like accounting, law, and engineering also have more graduates than the number of jobs available.[29] Considering the loans that most students have to repay, and the fact that many students are older and working their way through school, the starting salaries and the number of positions available are not encouraging.

High school graduates, particularly those looking for administrative jobs, are advised to enroll in training courses that teach computer applications. Temp agencies expect their workers to know at least four or five basic applications—a word-processing program like Word and WordPerfect, a spreadsheet application like Excel or Lotus, a database package like FoxPro—and to have some experience with desktop publishing and presentation graphics. Given the fact that there are semiannual software upgrades for each of these programs, and that programs rise and fall in popularity every few years, this places a daunting hurdle of training courses on the way to an administrative job. The problem is no less monumental for college graduates, who are also expected to keep their computer skills up to date.

Labor Secretary Robert Reich has repeatedly pointed to the widening wage gap between educated and uneducated workers, and the need to stress training to help bridge this gap. Entry into the secretarial workforce used to require stenographic, typing, and secretarial courses. And entry into more administrative positions has for the last decade or so generally required some college coursework, in addition to specific office skills. What has changed is that once again the "bar has been raised." More specific skills are required, more general education in the form of college level work is demanded, and more and more emphasis is placed on workers acquiring the skills themselves rather than having access to company-sponsored or government-supported programs. Indeed, in the freelance and temp world, training and educational expenses are expected to be shouldered by the individual. In keeping with the business philosophy behind reengineering, risks are to be taken by the individual, not the company.

JOB GROWTH?

In late 1994 and early 1995, company after company announced payroll reductions and the stock market responded by going up and up. Xerox Corporation, for example, reported that revenues were up significantly in 1994 while staff had been cut by 8 percent—or more than 7,000 people—since the previous year, and an additional 1,000 workers had been transferred to a subsidiary. This, like other company announcements, was good news to stockholders and those who play the stockmarket.

For Wall Street, payroll costs, including health and pension benefits and severance packages, have been treated as fixed expenses—they were commitments that the company could not operate without. Clearly this is no longer the case. While companies get tax write-offs, in the form of depreciation allowances, for investing in new equipment, payroll employees are treated as liabilities. Organizations are therefore investing heavily in office technology while shedding employee expenses. According to the Department of Commerce, business and consumer spending on high-tech equipment made up about 38 percent of economic growth since 1990.[30] Meanwhile, there are very few large companies that have not cut their payrolls. The list includes Apple, IBM, and Compaq among computer makers, AT&T and the regional phone companies, and Microsoft, the leader in the software industry. The white-collar world is now responding the way blue-collar manufacturing firms have since the 1980s.

In late 1994, there was much discussion about the decline in unemployment and the beginning of job growth. But although there are new jobs, they are in anything but permanent positions. Indeed, the growth in jobs, which actually began in 1993, is confined primarily to the service sector—the retail, fast food, cleaning, and health care fields, all of which use a large number of temporary and part-time workers. Few of the growth areas are in the office sector, and none are in manufacturing.

The three occupations that are projected to grow the most through the year 2005 are salespeople, registered nurses, and cashiers (see Figure 6.2).[31] Between 1992 and 1994, the company that added the largest number of jobs was Wal-Mart, the retail superstore.[32] Fourth in projected growth is the category of general office clerk, a grouping that lumps together all entry-level clerical support jobs. According to the Bureau of Labor Statistics' *Occupational Outlook Handbook,* its growth is expected to come from small businesses that hire a single worker to run the office—a trend that, as we can see from Figure 6.1, is not yet in evidence.[33] Tenth is computer systems analyst, a category that includes a wide

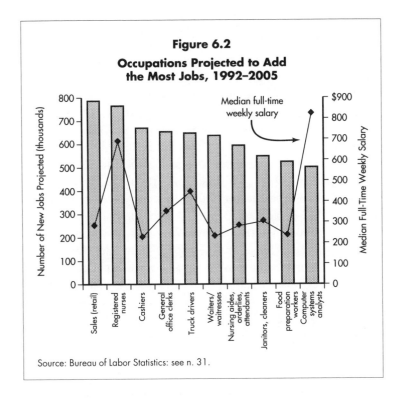

Figure 6.2

Occupations Projected to Add the Most Jobs, 1992–2005

Source: Bureau of Labor Statistics: see n. 31.

range of computer-related jobs. With the exception of registered nurses and computer systems analysts, *no* job growth is projected in any high-wage category or jobs offering the potential for full-time or semi-secure status.

While there is a demand for employees in the newer occupational groups in the computing field—network and database administrators, network technicians, and help-desk staff—this growth may turn out to be short-term. The new jobs have been created by the proliferation of networks, which has sparked the need to set standards for controlling files (administrators), to set-up network cabling and switching operations (technicians), and to staff the phones for people calling "help desks" when they run into problems.[34] Each of these computer-related tasks requires a high level of training and a large amount of on-the-job experience. The work meets the media image of high-tech, high-skill, comparatively high-paying work, but much of it is project-based and increasingly it is being done on a contingent basis. Further, median salaries for these workers have gone up only 4 percent since 1992, giving those systems analysts in full-time payroll jobs a median annual gross salary of $43,900.[35]

One of the myths about job creation is that while large companies are shedding their employees, small businesses are hiring. Yet the fact is that small businesses, particularly those with less than 100 employees, account for only a tiny percentage of total job growth.[36] In addition, more successful smaller firms, like those the Silicon Valley is known for, have relied on the deep pockets of the defense and aerospace industries and not on entrepreneurial strength. While small businesses hire workers at about twice the rate of larger ones, they also cut at a faster rate.[37]

This doesn't leave us with much to be optimistic about. A fundamental tenet of capitalism is that the efficiency of each company makes the overall economy more productive and competitive. At the root of this claim lies the belief that individual companies acting in their own self-interest will put steam into the economy, which will lead to economic growth and thus to job growth. But in the 1990s, neither economic growth nor job growth have followed this scenario. There is no engine pulling job growth, or, to use an information-age metaphor, the information superhighway seems to have bypassed the road that leads to growth in secure jobs.

7

SHAKING OFF
FALSE ASSUMPTIONS

Whether you're downsized or outsourced, whether you're fired or continue to work, it'll be under a completely different relationship—the idea of large numbers of white-collar people working in one corporation, moving up, and getting a pension is a phenomenon of the 1950s that is drawing to an end.

—*New York Times,* October 1994[1]

In *Alice in Wonderland,* Alice falls down a rabbit hole and finds a world that seems to follow different rules and be based on different assumptions. Although we didn't fall down a hole into the restructured world of work, understanding its rules and deciphering its assumptions is as daunting as the task that Alice encountered.

Much of the way we look at work, jobs, and technology is presented—in schools, at home, in the media, and in the academic and management literature—as conventional wisdom, sets of ideas that seem to be commonsense facts. In what follows, we will examine the developments described in earlier chapters in the wider context of economic and political policy in order to challenge this "common sense."

CONFRONTING CONVENTIONAL WISDOM

In the 1950s and 1960s, conventional wisdom claimed that the computer age would bring with it an information industry that would employ increasing numbers of well-paid white-collar workers. The message was spiced up in the 1970s and 1980s with a dash of high-tech dressing: technology would bring with it high-skill jobs that would be rewarded with high pay. Technology in general, and computers in particular, would bring forth a new future.

But as we have seen, conventional wisdom, particularly as presented through the nonanalytical lens of the popular media, is not always what it seems to be. Take, for example, the period from the 1950s through the 1980s, when office jobs were expanding. The office sector was what economists called a job-multiplier industry, creating enough jobs to offset the diminishing factory sector. We were told that this growth was fueled by the expansion of businesses that were competing effectively, even though much of it was the result of military and government spending. Even in the 1980s, despite the Reagan cutbacks, public sector jobs declined very little and military expenditures continued to support industrial companies with large white-collar payrolls.

But this is the 1990s, and there is no longer any magic pin holding office sector jobs in place. Political pressure to cut government and military spending, aided by workplace reengineering, have not simply "displaced" workers temporarily: the link between jobs and secure employment has been permanently cut.

The vestiges of the old factory-style division of labor and the early "automated" technology can still be seen in many jobs today, primarily because management policies—both the old-style "bureaucratic" and newer "humanistic" ones—laid the foundation for the separation between the head and the hands, and between the workplace and the worker. In other words, the "head" of company decision-making has been separated from the "hands" that do the work—anywhere. This is certainly not the scenario presented by business leaders when they claim that freeing business from the shackles of government regulation and public pressure is the best thing for everybody.

Yet conventional wisdom rests on the belief that business leaders know what is best for us, and this in turn is rooted in the assumption that unrestrained capitalist growth, supported by science and technology, will automatically lead to a growing economy, and to more and better jobs for those who are prepared for them. But this is no more than a technological leap of faith. After all, increased profits—the engine of growth—are the result of management's ability to decrease overall labor costs and make the labor process more controllable. Thus, as we have seen, more competitive *labor markets*, which hold wages down, and more streamlined *labor processes*, which press people to work harder and produce more quantifiable output, stand in stark contrast to the notion that increased competition is good for the worker in the workplace.

Capitalism, to be successful, must put profits ahead of people. But top managers who make decisions about profits are not omnipotent; nor are their plans always effective. In fact, their ability to control labor costs and introduce new forms of technology is curtailed by a number of factors that call into question the idea that technology "advances" in a straight line. The story of the writing tablet, in Chapter 3, illustrated how technology is not "invented" and then delivered to the workplace. The early writing tablet, like the palm-sized digital devices that are now being adopted, had to wait for the right economic conditions, appropriate forms of work organization, and developments in other areas of technology. Let's take these issues one at a time and, using history as a guide, see how they affect each other.

First, the early writing tablet was developed during a period of *economic expansion.* Many businesses, like the then perhaps over-confident IBM, were satisfied to leave well enough alone. Thus when the programmers said that they didn't see any need for such a device, the company, dependent on their skills, didn't push the new technology on them. Maybe the early tablet would not have been technically effective, or maybe it would have cost too much to make it fully reliable. In either case, there was at that time no particular economic justification for spending huge amounts to develop it further.

Second, in terms of *work organization,* large bureaucratic com-panies like IBM had well-established chains of command. Just as it was assumed that every manager needed a secretary, so it was also assumed that programmers gave their work to keypunch operators. The writing tablet was designed *before* terminals with keyboards (the precursor to the personal computer) were in widespread use, and people were not accustomed to entering and receiving data directly from the computer: the "normal" process was for the programmer to send information on paper to a keypunch operator, who punched it onto cards and sent them on to an operator who loaded them into input devices called card readers. This hierarchy was repeated in organization after orga-nization. Given the belief in bureaucratic principles, there was no particular reason for managers to shake up the hierarchy.

The third question focuses on *developments in other technolo-gies.* The writing tablet was designed to store data in the only type of computer known at that time—a centralized mainframe. Since only large organizations used computers, and since large organi-zations were bureaucratic, it was assumed that information had to be centrally collected and controlled.

Still another part of the story can be told by examining the *power relations* in the workplace. One thing that may have hin-dered the introduction of the writing tablet was the power of computer programmers in the 1960s and 1970s—they were in demand and their clout was felt up and down organizational hierarchies. And for programmers, as for managers, "things were okay the way they were."

Palm-sized computers, on the other hand, are being specially marketed to the mobile workforce—people who do not sit in offices and are perceived as working in isolation. Unlike the early writing tablet, which was locked into mainframe computer use, palm-sized computers are designed to fit in with a range of communication devices, from fax machines to mobile phones and pagers. In addition, they are being aimed at people who do not necessarily use computers and therefore won't insist on keeping things as they are.

The story is ongoing. New hardware and software is developed all the time, as are new management strategies for work organization. Sometimes the effectiveness of a new development is immediately apparent. Usually, however, there are power struggles and internal contradictions that need to be resolved before technology and work organization fit together. Workplace change is not passive, molded by "advancing technology" and top management.

To better understand how the design and introduction of technology are not inevitable, we now look at how we can challenge the conventional wisdom that is used to prop up the "American Dream."

IN SEARCH OF THE AMERICAN DREAM

According to the business press and popular wisdom, the new worker who wants to achieve the "American Dream" must be part of an entrepreneurial world: he or she is supposed to assume more risks, shoulder more responsibilities, and in general help the company become leaner and meaner in the race-course of international competition. But unlike the version of entrepreneurship that held sway in the last century, today's version doesn't have the worker owning much more than his or her own computer, or having much control over his or her earnings or working conditions. Indeed, many of the new "entrepreneurs" don't even wear a collar, let alone a white one—they work from home in t-shirts or sweatshirts.

If we go beyond the glowing talk of "technology as the wave of the future," we can see that many people are having trouble getting jobs, or keeping them—sprucing up their resumes each time the company reorganizes. These are not individual, personal problems but part of the restructured workplace.

The language of competition, combined with the ideology of individualism and professionalism, keeps office workers divided. Workers who believe that they must "work hard to get ahead" are pressured to constantly upgrade their skills, and as they work harder and harder, they may fail to notice that they, like millions of others, have been shunted off onto a side track—no longer part of an upwardly mobile path to increased responsibilities and wages. Instead of blaming managers, companies, and an economic system geared to make people compete, many workers end up blaming themselves. This too is no accident, but has been built into the white-collar workplace.

In the first two decades after World War II, a number of patterns of work relations were established in the United States. Some of these were shaped by progressive forces that sought to make the "American Dream" more equitable and secure. Social movements in the 1930s and 1940s had won social security for retired workers, unemployment insurance for laid-off workers, and public assistance for a wide range of people who couldn't work or didn't make enough to support themselves or their families. After congressional battles, Medicaid and Medicare were introduced in 1965 to provide health care for poor and low-waged people and for senior citizens. Unions were able to win higher wages and better health insurance, which the government and businesses agreed to help finance as long as the unions didn't demand wider changes—such as a voice in deciding technology or participation in management decisions.

But the white-collar middle class had little experience with unions, and seemed, according to media pronouncements, to be more interested in the "American Dream"—as promised by the various technological and information revolutions—than in fighting for social rights. As corporate employees, they bargained individually with their managers for higher salaries and annual increases. The belief was that if you were good, you would get ahead—an assumption built on the faith that office workers would be generously compensated for the skills they had acquired through education and experience. But although a small band of people were able to enter corporate and government jobs during the period of economic expansion, it took social policy in the form of affirmative action to pry open office doors for a wider range of workers, including women and minorities.

In order to sort through the rhetoric of the so-called American Dream, we need to question some of the basic assumptions that underly it. In the early part of this century, at the height of the industrial period, workers organized unions to fight for the collective rights of people working under one factory roof; these were later expanded into industry-wide unions. In the 1960s and 1970s, the beginning of the "post-industrial" period, people won civil and social rights in the midst of a rapidly changing economy. Now, as we enter yet another period of major upheaval, it is an open question whether the corporate short-term profit-taking can continue. The question is relevant for both managers and workers. For managers, the reengineering process has created a workforce that owes no particular allegiance to workplace or employer; for workers, the heightened competition has affected our health and our ability to spend time with our households. The urgency of this problem makes it especially necessary to question assumptions and plan new courses of action.

QUESTIONING ASSUMPTIONS

The media is fond of promoting the myth that the United States was founded on *individualism*. American expansionist policy used "individualism" as its theme, particularly in the push to settle the vast frontier. This image of the rugged individual carrying out his or her "advancement" was probably never applicable to the office worker—or any other worker, for that matter— but it continues to be used today, surprisingly effectively, within corporate walls. In fact, it is having a media rebirth as part of the push to get workers to work from home, much as the early pioneers were encouraged to spread out across the continent. And it is being used as part of the rush to encourage young people to become entrepreneurs—the ultimate image of the individual "out there on their own." While there is nothing wrong with a person trying to do his or her best and expecting to be rewarded for it, the problem is that individualism and professionalism are being bent out of shape, used primarily for the benefit of the organization, not the worker or customer.

It's not as if Americans are completely overwhelmed by the cult of individualism, of course. Outside of the workplace, we have a rich history of group action—from struggles over the environment to successful movements for women's rights and civil rights. In our schools, neighborhoods, communities, towns, cities, and regions, we have a track record of fighting to better our lives and the lives of our neighbors. What is unusual in the United States is that while this spirit of cooperative action—one that grows out of the same pioneer period that fostered individualism—has been extremely effective in changing the conditions and laws that affect our daily life, it is too often turned into a quest for individual advancement in the workplace.

Sociologists and anthropologists who study workplaces tell us that most work is done collectively, and that most office workers not only prefer to work together, but need to cooperate in order to accomplish such seemingly "routine" tasks as fixing the copier when the paper jams.[2] Office work, like most work, is by its very nature cooperative, and information work, with its heavy dependency on jumbles of software and hardware, is increasingly so. Asking a co-worker a question, sharing office stories, sorting out the mess of wires connecting the new local area network, and finding out how to transfer a message on the voice-mail system, are all best done with other people. Many people report that their first attempt at using "Windows" menus would have been nerve-racking without a co-worker leaning over their shoulder. We rely on each other for all sorts of information that makes our jobs more interesting and more productive.[3] Yet this web of cooperation disappears when the belief in individualism is brought to bear on negotiations with managers about salary increases or better work conditions.

C. Wright Mills wrote that technical and managerial jobs were built on the false assumption that the workers who held those jobs would inherit power in the office. But Mills noted that in fact moving up from the lower ranks of a corporate hierarchy was no more automatic than it had been for the working class in the industrial period to inherit the power to run the economy.[4] The linking of knowledge-based work with possible *power* is a purposely constructed illusion: the phrase "knowledge is power" does not translate into higher wages or better working conditions. Collectively shaking off these false assumptions, and reexamining some of the strong cooperative actions we have taken, may keep us from getting trapped in a future where we each have to bargain for some small piece of work—a world of individual freelancers competing against each other.

OPENING WINDOWS

Other "post-industrial" economies are doing things differently. The European Union, for example, has a Social Contract as part of its charter guaranteeing certain rights to working people. The U.S. Constitution, which fiercely guards *individual* freedoms, has no provisions that protect its citizens when they enter the workplace or contract with an employer.

Most Northern European countries guarantee access to free higher education, and also have retraining and apprenticeship programs, both for young people entering the labor market and for returning workers. U.S. Secretary of Labor Robert Reich has advocated similar retraining programs, but Congress, and even the President, have advocated cutting almost all such funding. In most other industrialized nations, education is financially secure—Israel, for example, despite its extraordinary military budget, puts education as its top financial priority. Yet in the United States, as taxes are reduced and funding slashed, the gap between rich and poor school districts has widened, threatening the education of more and more working-class and minority students, and spreading cuts through the middle class.

In the nineteenth and early twentieth centuries, the United States busily built a transportation infrastructure of railroads, subways, and trolley car lines. In New York City, for example, the subway was considered an important link for bringing workers inexpensively and effectively to their jobs. Now, however, the emphasis is moving away from public transportation and toward building highways for cars and the information superhighway for telecommunications. Both of these favor private infrastructure over public or mass facilities. In Europe and Japan, on the other hand, governments support revitalized rail transport, local public transportation systems, and publicly financed fiber optic networks.

Perhaps the most glaring difference between the United States and its close economic competitors is the lack of free and universal health care in the United States. While conservatives argue that Americans shouldn't lose the right to a "free choice of doctors," other nations have had comprehensive medical plans for several decades. And with the exception of England, where conservative politicians have whittled down the national health system, other countries let their citizens choose their own doctors. There are also free eye exams and occupational and physical therapy for people using computers.

Unemployment, a growing problem in all industrialized nations, is also handled differently in other countries. In France and Germany, for example, there are now proposals to cut the work week to four days while retaining a livable wage. In Norway, the exploitative nature of contingent work is being addressed through legislation that bans any work that does not guarantee the rights and pay of full-time employer-based work.

Decisions about technology in the workplace are another point of departure. When the Australian government wanted to revamp the tax collection system, it included representatives from the 18,000-member Taxation Office in an ongoing project to redesign jobs, develop new forms of work organization, and create new information systems. This large-scale undertaking was an attempt to avoid the pitfalls of top-down systems planning by relying on the active participation of workers from offices throughout the country. The public service employees union was included in the decision-making and, along with labor-oriented systems consultants, helped keep the project focused on the work that actually took place in the offices—not on management's vision of what they thought should happen. While cutting staff was one of the main objectives of the new system, the five-year phase-in of the new work organization and computer system was part of an agreement that allowed for only voluntary staff reductions. In addition, training in all aspects of the new job design was specifically mandated.

In Scandinavia, where the right of employees to "co-determine" technology policy dates back to the 1970s, laws and training workshops give workers the right to determine what type of technology is used in the workplace. This can take many forms, including unions and workers hiring their own consultants and choosing their own training and educational programs, but most importantly, co-determination boils down to the fact that hardware and software cannot be introduced in a workplace unless the workers agree to it.

Unions in the United States have failed to organize most of the office sector, and although there are many possible explanations for this—that they were too focused on male factory workers and not interested enough in female clerical office workers, for instance, and that they have been hamstrung by bureaucracies that mimic the companies they are bargaining against—the fact is that organizing against the power of individualism and the pressure of professionalism has not been an easy task. Large multinational white-collar employers like IBM, for example, had strict anti-union policies that they reinforced by emphasizing individual bargaining and making a cult of individualism and professionalism. Except for government employees, most white-collar workers in the United States are not unionized—unlike in the European Union, where almost all workers are represented by unions that not only bargain with specific employers, but also increase their bargaining power through country-wide negotiations.

Several U.S. unions have been moderately successful in shaking off their bureaucratic, top-heavy structure and making inroads in the office sector. The United Auto Workers (UAW) and the Communication Workers of America (CWA) have fought tough battles to secure the right to bargain collectively for their members. District 925 of the Service Employees International Union (SEIU), a newer union that grew out of the National Association of Working Women, has not only pushed for collective bargaining but has also played a strong role in educating office workers about their rights.

Collective bargaining, while tied up in thousands of industrial-based rules and regulations, presents an important contrast to individualism. As its name implies, it is based on the idea that *collectives*, or groups of people, have potentially more clout than individuals, particularly when it comes to negotiations over salaries, benefits, and working conditions. The lone individual going to his or her boss and asking for a raise based on individual performance stands little chance compared to groups collectively arguing for better pay and conditions based on what they as a group accomplish. In fact, the corporate emphasis on team and group work is strangely out of sync with the cult of individualism, yet individualism in this sphere prevails because companies want to keep it that way. Since most office workers bargain for themselves without knowing what their co-workers earn, the organization holds the cards.

Unions as they were known in the industrial period may not be the answer for collective bargaining in the rapidly changing office sector today. And European white-collar unions, with their history of national collective action, may not be an appropriate response to the long American tradition of isolating individuals. There are other alternatives, however, such as the European worker councils, which are mandated by law to collectively bargain with employers on the local level. In the United States before industrial unionism, there were non-workplace-based unions that served the interests of groups of workers. Waitresses, for example, had a strong association that trained and provided workers for the vast restaurant industry. Such a model might well work among non-workplace-based office workers. The Industrial Workers of the World is starting an employee-run temporary agency in San Francisco that is to serve as a hiring hall for the growing temporary work sector. And on a political level, it has been suggested that employee lobbies could help to counteract the power of the employer lobbies that now dominate Capitol Hill.

Whatever strategies we adopt to reshape worker-management relations, it is clear that a worker's right to healthy, safe working conditions and a living wage must be negotiated within a framework that re-balances the power of workers against the growing power of employers. The American Dream cannot stop at the office door. A recent government study found that more than 80 percent of workers want to have some say in the decisions that affect their jobs and in how their work is performed.[5] Watering down existing health and safety regulations, or taking away legislation that protects unions and workers, is not only a step backward, but seriously endangers the millions of Americans working outside offices and outside traditional employer-employee contractual agreements.

Clearly, we can't go backward. Instead we must build on the collective practices that have been successfully used in the past. We have been bombarded with a conventional wisdom that makes it appear that technological revolutions and free-market business policies will lead to a better future. In the 1990s, we have had a glimpse of this future and it has not been designed for or by us. But, as our counterparts in earlier periods of major economic change have shown, we too can influence the direction of change. The more we as workers and citizens collectively question the way things are, the more possibilities there will be for us to shape the way things could be, from the technology we use to the way we organize our work.

EPILOGUE: DOWNSIZING

The Queen Bee Circle,

The policymaking wing of the honey bee industry, announced today
it has come to an agreement with major hives
to reduce the number of worker bees in order to increase
the short-term ratio of milliliter of honey per worker bee.

The Queen Bees have also voted themselves more Royal Jelly
to reflect their increased responsibilities.
Layoffs will be accomplished through attrition
and kicking the workers out of the hive to starve or freeze.

Wall Street responded enthusiastically; sweetener stocks soared.
Washington is concerned about a reaction from environmental
groups, since experts predict there will never be wildflowers
in American meadows or roadsides again.

Aphrodite, foam-born Goddess of Love,

called a press conference. Citing disappointing fourth-quarter results,
she announced plans to cut Cupid staff to the bone.

"These are the 1990s," announced the tautly muscled goddess,
"and we're cutting out the flab. We can't afford benefits like ecstasy."
Industry prognosticators forecast whoopee only on weekends.
Record companies immediately cancelled love tunes.

Wrap up: unless something is done,
teenagers in love will have to get used to colder nights
and bleaker days, silent airwaves and part-time drudgery.

Good night and have a pleasant tomorrow.

Daniel Caplice Lynch
West Lebanon, New York

NOTES

NOTES TO CHAPTER 1

1. George is a made-up name, as are the names of all the people in the stories that follow. Unless otherwise specified, the stories and anecdotes are based on two dozen in-depth interviews conducted in late 1993 and throughout 1994 with a wide range of white collar workers at their work sites. The interviewees were selected to represent different occupational categories, firm sizes, and employment relations. Follow-up interviews were conducted by telephone. In addition, I interviewed ten high-level managers from different types of large firms, including telecommunications, computers, banks, and staffing agencies. The survey cannot be considered statistically representative of today's white collar occupations, but it was designed on the basis of an analysis of available literature on these occupations.

2. According to the U.S. Department of Labor, *Employment and Earnings*, January 1995, Table 11, Household Data Annual Averages, Employed Civilians by Detailed Occupation, the following are included as full- and part-time workers:

Executive, administrative, and managerial	16,312,000
Professional specialities	17,536,000
Technical and related support	3,869,000
Administrative support, including clerical	18,620,000
Total Executive, Professional, Technical, Admin.	56,337,000
Total employed over 16 years (total labor force)	123,050,000

Professional specialties in health, such as nurses and doctors, as well as teachers, and such technical jobs as clinical laboratory technicians are generally considered white collar, although they may not necessarily be "office" jobs. For the purposes of this book, white collar and office jobs include the four major occupational categories listed above. These categories do not include: Sales, with 14,817,000 workers; Service (including household), with 16,912,000; or Craft and Factory operators.

3. Adapted from Roger Swardson, "In One Office, the Toll of a New Machine," *Washington Post*, 5 September 1993, pp. C1, C4.

4. U.S. Department of Labor, Bureau of Labor Statistics, Monthly Household Surveys, April 1995.

5. The Bureau of Labor Statistics has redesigned the Current Population Survey. See U.S. Department of Labor, *Monthly Labor Review* (September 1993), for articles discussing the changes that have been made in the survey. The redesign includes new questions asking if people are employed in the home or if they are self-employed. Some of these workers were previously counted as unemployed, and some, particularly women, were counted as not being in the labor force. Contingent work is discussed in Chapters 5 and 6.

6. See Mathew Jones, "Don't Emancipate, Exaggerate: Rhetoric, Reality and Reengineering," in R.L. Berskenke et al., eds., *Information Technology and New Emergent Forms of Organizations* (Amsterdam: Elsevier, 1994).

7. Michael Hammer, "Reengineering Work: Don't Automate, Obliterate," *Harvard Business Review* (July-August 1990): 104; italics added.

8. See *Webster's New Twentieth Century Dictionary* (New York: Collins, 1979).

9. Bureau of Labor Statistics, Monthly Household Surveys, April 1995.

10 See computer magazines like *PC World, Mac World,* and *Home Office,* as well as journals like *Communications of the Association for Computing Machinery*. For business coverage, see *Business Week, Forbes, Fortune,* and the *Harvard Business Review.*

11 Phil Patton, "The Virtual Office Becomes Reality," *New York Times,* 28 October 1993, p. C1.

12 Daniel Bell, *The Coming of the Post-Industrial Society* (New York: Basic Books, 1976).

13 Edward Tenner, "The Paradoxical Proliferation of Paper," *Harvard Magazine* (March-April 1988): 23-26.

NOTES TO CHAPTER 2

1. C. Wright Mills, *White Collar* (New York: Oxford University Press, 1951), preface, p. x.

2. For a discussion of the transformation of factory work, see Harley Shaiken, *Work Transformed* (New York: Holt, Rinehart and Winston, 1984), and Barry Bluestone and Bennett Harrison, *The Deindustrialization of America* (New York: Basic Books, 1982).

3. Mills, *White Collar*, p. 63.

4. See, for example, Teresa Amott, *Caught in the Crisis: Women and the U.S. Economy Today* (New York: Monthly Review Press, 1993).

5. See Ellen Lupton, *Mechanical Brides: Women and Machines from Home to Office* (New York: Princeton Archectural Press, 1993), p. 43.

6. Items in the box are from U.S. Congress, Office of Technology Assessment, *Automating America's Offices* (Washington, DC: 1985); Lupton, *Mechanical Brides*; and Marjorie Wolfe, "But How Fast Can You Type, Sir," *New York Times,* 22 May 1994, p. B10.

7. Lupton, *Mechanical Brides*, p. 44.

8. Mary Murphree, "Brave New Office: The Changing World of the Legal Secretary," in Karen Sacks and Dorothy Remy, eds., *My Troubles Are Going to Have Trouble with Me* (New Brunswick, NJ: Rutgers University Press, 1984); see also Mary Murphree, "New Technology and Office Tradition: The No-so-changing World of the Secretary," in Heidi Hartmann et al., eds., *Computer Chips and Paper Clips,* Vol. II (Washington, DC: National Academy Press, 1987).

9. Barbara Garson, *The Electronic Sweatshop* (New York: Penguin Books, 1988).

10 Juliette Webster, *Office Automation: The Labour Process and Women's Work in Britain* (London: Harvester Wheatsheaf, 1993), p. 118.

11 Joan Greenbaum, *In the Name of Efficiency: Management Theory and Shopfloor Practice in Data-Processing Work* (Philadelphia, PA: Temple University Press, 1979).

12 Ibid., p. 65.

13 Ibid., p. 64.

14 R. Boguslaw, *The New Utopians: A Study of System Design and Social Change* (Englewood Cliffs, NJ: Prentice-Hall, 1965), p. 2.

NOTES TO CHAPTER 3

1. U.S. Department of Health, Education, and Welfare, Special Taskforce Report, *Work in America* (Cambridge, MA: MIT Press, 1973), p. 38.

2. Greenbaum, *In the Name of Efficiency,* p. 29.

3. Pelle Ehn, *Work-Oriented Design of Computer Artifacts* (Hillside, NJ: Lawrence Erlbaum Assoc., 1990).

4. Russell Ackoff, *Redesigning the Future: A Systems Approach to Societal Programs* (New York: Wiley, 1974), p. 8.

5. In the early 1970s, when I was a systems consultant for the Bureau of Child Welfare in New York City, I saw first hand the effect that system design had on cutting recipients out of social services and cutting social work up into parts. During this period, welfare roles were growing and government agencies were looking for new ways to cut the costs of processing and providing services. Ross Perot, for example, made a fortune by winning the contracts to process the welfare checks in most states. He claimed that his firm could do it for less. Meanwhile, in New York City in the late 1960s, social workers struck to try to stop the division of labor and the deskilling that the new systems were bringing to their profession.

6. See Greenbaum, *In the Name of Efficiency.*

7. Engineers that I have spoken to recently have said that an input device for handwriting with close to 90 percent accuracy would not have been likely in 1968. Since the project was secret at the time, there is no way to go back and confirm how dependable or accurate it was, but the point here is that it was certainly far enough along for marketing studies to begin, and far enough along for management to be making plans to take it "from the lab" to some practical application.

8. Items in this box are from Heidi Hartmann et al., eds., *Computer Chips and Paper Clips,* Vol. I (Washington, DC: National Academy Press, 1986), p. 26; Greenbaum,

In the Name of Efficiency, p. 26; Tenner, "The Paradoxical Proliferation of Paper," p. 3.

9. Richard Edwards, *Contested Terrain: The Transformation of the Workplace in the Twentieth Century* (New York: Basic Books, 1979). p. 21.

10. U.S. Department of Health, Education, and Welfare, *Work in America,* pp. 48, 44.

11. Harry Braverman, *Labor and Monopoly Capital: The Degradation of Work in the Twentieth Century* (New York: Monthly Review Press, 1974), p. 126.

12. Ibid., passim.

13. For some much-read management books of the period see, for example, Alfred Chandler, *Strategy and Structure* (Cambridge, MA: MIT Press, 1962); Herbert Simon, *The Shape of Automation for Men and Management* (New York: Harper & Row, 1965); and Peter F. Drucker, *Technology, Management, and Society* (New York: Harper & Row, 1970).

14. Braverman, *Labor and Monopoly Capital,* pp. 39, 37.

15. Cited in ibid., p. 112, 113, 119, from Frederick Taylor, *Scientific Management* (New York: Harper, 1947).

16. Studs Terkel, *Working* (New York: Avon, 1972), p. 139.

17. Ibid., p. 141.

18. U.S. Department of Health, Education, and Welfare, *Work in America,* p. 40.

19. To a certain extent, the same case could be made for factory work—namely that skill cannot be made into simple repetitive tasks, and that in many of the cases where this was done, worker resistance took the steam of out managerial control.

20. Greenbaum, *In the Name of Efficiency,* p. 19.

NOTES TO CHAPTER 4

1. Quoted in Shoshana Zuboff, *In the Age of the Smart Machine: The Future of Work and Power* (New York: Basic Books, 1988), p. 139.

2. See, for example, T. Peters and R. Waterman, *In Search of Excellence: Lessons from America's Best-Run Companies* (New York: Harper & Row, 1982).

3. Office of Technology Assessment, *Automating America's Offices,* pp. 117-18; italics added.

4. *Forbes,* 29 March 1993, p. 49. It is difficult to find reliable figures on the number of PCs in use, especially since almost all the data comes from companies that make hardware and software.

5. Andrew Friedman, *Computer Systems Development: History, Organization, and Implementation* (New York: Wiley, 1989).

6. Joan Greenbaum and Morten Kyng, eds., *Design at Work: Cooperative Design of Computer Systems* (Hillsdale, NJ: Erlbaum Associates, 1991).

7. Liam Bannon, "From Human Factors to Human Actors," in ibid.

8. E. Yourdon, *Managing the Structured Techniques* (New York: Yourdon Press, 1986), p. 61.

9. Susanne Bødker, Joan Greenbaum, and Morten Kyng, "Situated Design," in Greenbaum and Kyng, eds., *Design at Work.*

10. Zuboff, *In the Age of the Smart Machine,* p. 57.

11. Garson, *Electronic Sweatshop,* p. 45.

12. Juliette Schor, *The Overworked American* (New York: Basic Books, 1991).

13. See Office of Technology Assessment, *Automating America's Offices.*
14. See, for example, Zuboff, *In the Age of the Smart Machine,* and Paul Adler, "New Technologies, New Skills," *California Management Review* 29, no. 1 (Fall 1986).
15. Robert Howard, *Brave New Workplace* (New York: Viking, 1985), p. 111.
16. Ibid., p. 112.
17. Ibid.; italics added.
18. U.S. Department of Labor, Bureau of Labor Statistics, *Household Surveys,* January 1983, Table 23.
19. Zuboff, *In the Age of the Smart Machine,* p. 170.
20. Sharon Szymanski, "Unrequited Skills: The Effect of Technology on Clerical Work," Ph.D. diss., New School for Social Research, 1989; available from University Microfilms, Ann Arbor, Michigan.
21. Office of Technology Assessment, *Automation of America's Offices,* p. 19.

NOTES TO CHAPTER 5

1. Quoted in Amalia Duarte, "Workers and AT&T Both Grapple with the Reality of Layoffs," *New York Times,* 28 August 1994, New Jersey Section, p. 1.
2. Quoted in Louis Uchitelle, "The Rise of the Losing Class," *New York Times,* 20 November 1994, Section 4, p. 1.
3. Ibid.
4. At present the Bureau of Labor Statistics does not keep track of Customer Service Representatives as a separate category. According to the BLS's *Occupational Outlook Handbook,* these workers are included under a number of different job descriptions, including the growing category of Information Clerks, which includes Credit Clerks and New Account Clerks.
5. Richard Karlgaard, *Forbes ASAP,* 7 December 1992, p. 9.
6. Szymanski, "Unrequited Skills," particularly chapters 1 and 2.
7. See, for example, Hartmann et al., eds., *Computer Chips and Paper Clips,* Vols. I and II; see also Murphree, "Brave New Office: The Changing Role of the Legal Secretary," and Lucy Suchman and Eleanor Wynn, *Procedures and Problems in the Office Environment* (Palo Alto, CA: Xerox Advanced Systems Department, 1979).
8. "High performance" workplaces are stressed in business and government reports. A good overview and interpretation of what this means for office workers can be found in 9 to 5, Working Women Education Fund, *High Performance Office Work: Improving Jobs and Productivity* (Cleveland, OH: 9 to 5, 1992).
9. See, for example, *Income, Earnings and Jobs: Findings from the New Edition of the State of Working America* (Washington, DC: Economic Policy Insitute, 1994); *Fact-Finding Report: Commission on the Future of Worker-Management Relations* [Dunlop Report] (Washington, DC: U.S. Department of Labor, 1994); *On Shaky Ground: Rising Fears about Incomes and Earnings* (Washington, DC: National Commission for Employment Policy, 1994).
10. See Szymanski, "Unrequited Skills"; as well as Sharon Hartman Strom, *Beyond the Typewriter: Gender, Class, and the Origins of Modern American Office Work, 1890-1930* (Urbana, IL: University of Illinois Press, 1992) and Hartmann et al., eds., *Computer Chips and Paper Clips,* vols. I and II.
11. *Business Week,* 1 August 1994, p. 14.

12. Louis Uchitelle, "New Economy Dashes Old Notions of Growth," *New York Times,* 27 November 1994, p. B1.

13. This issue of replacing employees with equipment is an often repeated theme in the *New York Times* and *Wall Street Journal.* It has also been featured in cover stories about jobs in *Business Week,* 17 October 1994; *Fortune,* 19 September 1994; and *Time,* 22 November 1993.

14. See Janice Horowitz, "Crippled by Computers," *Time,* 12 October 1992; see also Peter T. Kilborn, "Workplace Injury Is Rising, and the Computer Is Blamed," *New York Times,* 16 December 1989; *A Price for Every Progress: The Hazard of VDTs* (video) (New York: Labor Institute, 1988).

15. See Jonathan Bennett, "How Safe Are They?" *Microwave News,* November 1990; see also the Labor Institute's video and workbook, *Hazards of the Modern Office: EMFs* (New York: Labor Institute, 1993); *Electric and Magnetic Fields and Your Health,* a report of the Working Group of Electiric and Magnetic ELF Fields (Toronto: Department of Health and Welfare, 1989); Paul Brodeur, "Annals of Radiation: The Hazards of Electromagnetic Fields," *The New Yorker,* 12 June 1989.

16. Aaron Berstein, "Inequality: How the Gap Between Rich and Poor Hurts the Economy," *Business Week,* 15 August 1994, p. 78.

17. In "In Race to Fiscal Recovery, Southeast Is a Dazzling Pacesetter," *New York Times,* 27 November 1993, p. 8.

18. See Virginia du Rivage, ed., *New Policies for the Part-Time and Contingent Workforce* (Armonk, NY: M.E. Sharpe, 1992); Robert Calem, "Working at Home, for Better or Worse," *New York Times,* 18 April 1993, Section 3, p. 1.

19. Quoted in Steven Prokesch, "Service Jobs Fall as Business Gains," *New York Times,* 18 April 1993, p. 43.

20. Barbara Presley Noble, "Must It Be No Pain, No Gain?" *New York Times,* 8 May 1994, Business Section, p. 23.

21. Peter Kilborn, "More Women Take Low-wage Jobs Just So Their Families Can Get By," *New York Times,* 13 March 1994, p. 24.

22. U.S. Department of Labor, Bureau of Labor Statistics, Current Population Survey, Household Data, 1994.

23. Quoted in Stanley Aronowitz and William Di Fazio, *The Jobless Future* (Minneapolis, MN: University of Minnesota Press, 1994), p. 82.

24. Census Bureau data cited in Berstein, "Inequality: How the Gap Between Rich and Poor Hurts the Economy," p. 78.

NOTES TO CHAPTER 6

1. Quoted in "The New World of Work," *Business Week,* Special Report, 65th Anniversary Issue, 17 October 1994, p. 86.

2. William Bridges, "The End of the Job," *Fortune,* 19 September 1994, pp. 62-74.

3. George J. Church, "Jobs in an Age of Insecurity," *Time,* 22 November 1993, pp. 34-38.

4. "Business Rolls the Dice," *Business Week,* 65th Anniversary Issue, 17 October 1994, p. 89.

5. Jaclyn Fierman, "The Contingency Work Force," *Fortune,* 24 January 1994, pp.

30-36; see also U.S. Department of Labor, Bureau of Labor Statistics, "Help Supply Services," monthly data (SIC code 7363).

6. Fierman, "The Contingency Work Force," p. 31; figures for the IBM and Ford domestic workforces are from 1994 Fortune 500 data.

7. *Business Week,* 19 September 1994, p. 27.

8. Quoted in Fierman, "The Contingency Work Force," p. 32.

9. Quoted in "Execu-Temps," *Continental Airlines Profile Magazine,* April 1994, p. 18.

10. Kirk Johnson, "Evolution of the Workplace Alters Office Relationships," *New York Times,* 5 October 1994, p. B1.

11. "The New World of Work," p. 85.

12. Fierman, "The Contingency Work Force," p. 32.

13. Eileen Appelbaum and Rosemary Batt, *The New American Workplace: Transforming Work Systems in the United States* (Ithaca, NY: ILR Press, 1994).

14. Eileen Appelbaum, "Structural Change and the Growth of Part-Time and Temporary Employment," in du Rivage, ed., *New Policies for the Part-Time and Contingent Workforce,* p. 4.

15. Chris Tilly, "Short Hours, Short Shrift," in du Rivage, ed., *New Policies for the Part-Time and Contingent Workforce,* p. 19; see also Polly Callaghan and Heidi Hartmann, *Contingent Work: A Chart Book on Part-Time and Temporary Employment* (Washington, DC: Economic Policy Insitute, 1991).

16. U.S. Department of Labor, Bureau of Labor Statistics, Monthly Household Surveys, 1994. For an analysis of new part-time data collection methods, see Anne Polivka and Jennifer Rothgeb, "Redesigin the CPS Questionnaire," *Monthly Labor Review,* September 1993.

17. Quoted in Fierman, "The Contingency Work Force," p. 33.

18. See Robert Calem, "Working at Home, for Better or Worse," *New York Times,* 18 April 1993, Section 3, p. 1; see also Fierman, "The Contingency Work Force."

19. See, for example, U.S. House of Representatives, *High-Tech and Low-Wage,* Report of the Communication Workers of America for the Committee on Government Operations (Washington, DC: 1993); see also Pamela Mario, "The Use of Information Technology and Its Relationship to Job Characteristics of Administrative Support Personnel," *Office Systems Research Journal,* Spring 1993.

20. Schor, *The Overworked American.*

21. From Swardson, "In One Office, the Toll of a New Machine," p. C1.

22. See Jeremy Rifkin, *End of Work* (Rutherford, NJ: Putnam, 1995).

23. This data, as well as the material in Figure 6.1, is from U.S. Department of Labor, Bureau of Labor Statistics, Table 56, Household Data Annual Averages, Full-Time Workers, 1990, 1992, 1993. Table 56 was renumbered Table 39 in 1994, but the data is comparable for these positions. In *Employment and Earnings* (January 1995).

24. Anthony Ramirez, "NYNEX to Cut 22% of Work Force," *New York Times,* 25 January 1994, p. D1.

25. See note 23.

26. Robert Lewis, "Downsizing Victims Tackle Range of Woes," *AARP Bulletin* 36, no. 2 (February 1995): 1.

27. See note 23.

28. "College Grads in Tight Market," *Arizona Republic,* 17 April 1994, p. D6.

29. Peter T. Kilborn, "College Seniors Find More Jobs but Modest Pay," *New York*

Times, 1 May 1994, p. 1; see also Tamar Lewin, "Low Pay and Closed Doors Greet Young in Job Market," *New York Times,* 10 March 1994, p. 1.
30. Michael Mandel, "The Digital Juggernaut," *Business Week,* Special 1994 Bonus Issue on "The Information Revolution," p. 22.
31. These statistics and those in Figure 6.2 are from Bureau of Labor Statistics data in *The American Workforce, 1992-2005.* See also Peter T. Kilborn, "Job Security Hinges on Skills, Not on Employer for Life," *New York Times,* 12 March 1994, p. 1.
32. Sylvia Nasar, "Myth: Small Businesses as Job Engine," *New York Times,* 25 March 1994, p. D1.
33. According to the *Occupational Outlook Handbook,* General Office Clerks are entry-level people who are hired to run all types of small offices, from doctors' offices to wholesale firms.
34. The Bureau of Labor Statistics has not as yet broken the category of Systems Analyst down into the newly emerging job categories, which are all lumped together under Computer Systems Analysts and Scientists. This may be the reason why this single category seems to be growing so rapidly. See the BLS's *Occupational Outlook Handbook* for a full description of this job category.
35. See note 23.
36. Bennett Harrison, *Lean and Mean: The Changing Landscape of Corporate Power in the Age of Flexibility* (New York: Basic Books, 1994).
37. Nasar, "Myth: Small Businesses as Job Engine," p. D1.

NOTES TO CHAPTER 7

1. Johnson, "Evolution of the Workplace Alters Office Relationships," p. B1.
2. Lucy Suchman, *Plans and Situated Actions* (New York: Cambridge University Press, 1987).
3. See, for example, Zuboff, *In the Age of the Smart Machine.*
4. Mills, *White Collar.*
5. *Fact-Finding Report: Commission on the Future of Worker-Management Relations* [Dunlop Report].

INDEX